FOUNDATION STONE

FOUNDATION STONE

Notes Towards a Constitution For a 21st-Century Republic

Theo Dorgan, editor

FOUNDATION STONE
First published 2014
by New Island
2 Brookside
Dundrum Road
Dublin 14
www.newisland.ie

PRINT ISBN: 978-1-84840-259-1
EPUB ISBN: 978-1-84840-260-7
MOBI ISBN: 978-1-84840-261-4

British Library Cataloguing Data. A CIP catalogue record for this book is available from the British Library

Typeset by Mariel Deegan
Cover design by Mariel Deegan
printed by Scandbook AB, Sweden

New Island received financial assistance from the Western Development Commission.

10 9 8 7 6 5 4 3 2 1

CONTENTS

Acknowledgements

The editor and the publisher wish to acknowledge with gratitude a generous contribution from the Western Development Commission towards the costs of this publication.

We wish also to acknowledge the facilitation of this project by Roscommon County Council; their long-standing commitment to the Douglas Hyde Conference has for many years made a profound contribution to public debate in Ireland.

Three Prefaces

1.

The 2012 Douglas Hyde Conference marked the twenty-fourth consecutive year in which this conference has been held in County Roscommon. Its enduring legacy can be attributed to the cherished position that the figure of Douglas Hyde holds in the consciousness of the people of his native Roscommon, the significant contribution he made to the cultural narrative of this country and his role as the first president of Ireland. The annual conference fulfils a key function in honouring and commemorating his achievements.

The conference is an important and integral part of our cultural calendar of events and arts programming, and down through the years has been a forum for discussion on a range of issues that have informed national debate. The 2012 conference, with its focused theme of 'A Constitution for a 21st-Century Republic', in relation to the Constitutional Convention, continued that strong programming tradition. The subject resonated with a broad audience and attracted a distinguished line-up of leading thinkers, academics, commentators and speakers.

Of the many issues discussed at the conference, a recurring concern expressed by speakers and the audience was that knowledge, learning and discussion in relation to the Constitutional Convention should be brought into the public domain. The papers contained in this publication reflect the many opposing and strong viewpoints expressed on the Constitutional Convention proposals, which will undoubtedly enlighten and interest many readers and stimulate further debate.

This publication offers an opportunity, therefore, to situate such deliberations within the context of a wider national audience and increase dialogue. It also highlights the important information role that the conference continues to play in steering issues in new and meaningful directions.

We welcome this publication of the Douglas Hyde Conference Proceedings 2012. I would like to take this opportunity to thank all the contributors who have agreed to make their papers available for publication. We would like to thank, and acknowledge the work of, the convenor and chair Mr Theo Dorgan.

Frank Dawson
County Manager
Roscommon County Council

2.

The Western Development Commission (WDC) was delighted to partner once again with Roscommon County Council in hosting the 2012 Douglas Hyde Conference. The conference plays a very important role in providing a platform from which to rigorously analyse pressing issues that affect not only the people of the West of Ireland, but the entire nation. The 2012 conference marked a substantial shift in theme from recent years, where the place of creative industries within wider society was examined, towards an interrogation of the Constitutional Convention.

This year's conference papers provide testament to the depth and quality of debate for which the Douglas Hyde Conference has become renowned. The WDC is very proud to be associated with this publication, as it provides a window into the creative and enquiring minds of the people of the Western Region who seek a better future for wider society through the collaborative efforts of all who share our vision for the region.

The WDC would like to extend its appreciation to Mr Richie Farrell of Roscommon County Council, who organised the conference, to Mr Theo Dorgan for convening and chairing the conference, and to New Island for the production of these insightful papers.

Ian Brannigan
Chief Executive
Western Development Commission

3.

It has been a signal pleasure and an honour for some years now to have been invited to act as convenor and chair of the annual Douglas Hyde Conference. The Conference has served to raise many important national issues, attracting contributors of the highest calibre, whose talks, debates and performances have immeasurably enriched the national conversation at a time when our country is undergoing a succession of shocks and changes in all spheres of the national life. Many of the themes first examined and debated at the Conference over the years have gone on to inform and stimulate national thinking in the arenas of arts, politics, social justice and culture, so much so that some scholar of the future will be able to trace the emergence of much important new thinking on these themes to successive Douglas Hyde Conferences.

It has been a source of some regret to the organisers, to the contributors and indeed to myself that reporting on each year's Conference has been so scant. I hope that this is not due to some metropolitan bias, and even more I hope that it is not due to some received media wisdom that the Irish people have no real interest in matters cultural and intellectual. Those of us who have had the good fortune to be present at the Conference down the years have had the privilege of listening to many of the most important and challenging scholars, intellectuals and artists of our time at the height of their powers. Their passionate and insightful contributions have stimulated, informed and cheered audiences as diverse as any gathering in Ireland might be – audiences, I might add, who have never been slow to join in debate, often to considerable enlightening effect.

The 2012 Conference addressed the theme: 'A Constitution for a 21st-Century Republic'. Such was the quality and range of perspectives offered by a very distinguished panel of scholars, and such is the importance in the present moment of widening out debate on the Constitution, that I thought it important to find some way to bring the contributions to a wider audience. I am grateful to New Island Books for agreeing with such enthusiasm to publish the proceedings, despite the fact that this book had not figured in their budget projections for 2013, and to the Western Development Commission for offering so generously to assist in defraying the costs of the publication. I am particularly grateful to the contributors who were kind enough to waive the fees they might legitimately have expected, so that this book and its arguments might be placed before the wider public at this critical time. More than this, of course, I am grateful to them for the depth and breadth of scholarship and thought that each of them has brought to bear on their respective contributions.

I should point out that, in order to stake out the ground of debate as comprehensively as possible, I invited Orla O'Connor of the National Women's Council of Ireland to add one further essay to the original Conference contributions; pressure of time in the run-up to the Conference meant it was not possible to invite her participation then.

It is a considerable tribute to the vision of Roscommon County Council that this Conference continues to go from strength to strength. We are very much in the debt of the Council, the County Manager Frank Dawson, County Librarian Richie Farrell and the former Arts

Officer Philip Delamere for their unswerving commitment to the Conference down through the years.

I should make it plain that this collection of essays embraces a wide range of views on how we should provide for ourselves, in terms of a Constitution, in the coming years. I have my own views on this, and in my introduction I express some of those views as clearly and explicitly as I can; nevertheless, it seems to me more important at this moment that we consider as many different points of view as might reasonably be gathered into one modest book.

Between us all, we hope that the papers collected here will serve to inform, challenge and bring light to bear on a central question for our times: how should we constitute ourselves as a republic in the twenty-first century?

Theo Dorgan

INTRODUCTION

Theo Dorgan

1.

The fundamental compact that legitimates the State on the one hand, and on the other hand enlists us all as citizens in the functioning and governance of the political process, is, or should be, the Constitution. It seems reasonable to argue that the Constitution is the reification as a document of a collective act of self-definition, the act of constituting ourselves; as such it should reflect our values, provide for our liberties, offer guidelines for legislation, act to protect us from tyranny and represent us as a people to other peoples and to other states. Carefully considered and enacted by ourselves, the Constitution should above all else be sufficient for the great purposes of justice, equality and solidarity.

When this is not the case, when objective internal and external conditions have so far changed as to make it prudent and necessary to develop a new charter for our polity, then it would be wise and an exercise in statecraft to hold a root-and-branch inquiry into the Constitution in its entirety.

Externally, the most important political development we need to accommodate is the European Union. Without going into the matter too deeply for the moment, it seems to me that our membership of the Union continues to disclose new obligations, new limits to sovereignty and new circumscriptions on our freedom to act in our own best interests, and on those grounds alone I would argue that we need a thorough overhaul of the Constitution in order to more clearly define our relationship to emerged and emerging phenomena of the realpolitik. In theory, the EU is a free union of sovereign states, pooling their sovereignties and acting in concert; in practice, such is the present unwieldiness of the Union, we are evolving rapidly towards a very different future for the European project, something far more like a superstate than a union. If this is indeed the future to which we have wittingly or unwittingly mortgaged ourselves, then our Constitution is in need of an urgent overhaul – the disjunction between the constitution appropriate to a sovereign state and the constitution appropriate to a satrap or vassal state is that large.

Internally, the absolute ceding of our sovereignty by the present and the immediately preceding governments yields another argument for overhauling the Constitution – if sovereignty can be ceded by the Parliament, and this yielding of sovereignty is not accepted by the mass of the people as legitimate, as there are good grounds to suspect is not the case, then the Constitution does not act as a brake on executive powers as it should, or else it provides for those powers in a way that no constitution of a democratic republic should.

All of which leads me to say that the Constitutional Convention as at present conceived is a very odd beast indeed.

This exercise, set in train by Taoiseach Enda Kenny, has drawn three main strands of response: the Government and its boot-strappers think, vaguely, that it's probably a good thing, or at least incapable of causing much harm, but of marginal political importance; many seasoned commentators think it marginal also, but tend to see it more as a missed opportunity, and dubious too: though the Convention has been asked to look at the role of the Seanad, for instance, and report their views on it, at the same time the Taoiseach has blithely announced that he intends to abolish the second chamber anyway – which makes one wonder if there is any point to the exercise at all; the third strand, and this is the one that should give most cause for concern, not least because it is far and away the most populous, is made up of those for whom the entire exercise is a matter of indifference.

I say that this strand gives most cause for concern because it is yet another manifestation of the withdrawal of much of the population from the political process. As it seems to most people now, though they might not formulate it as I do, the professional political class and its elite allies have taken ownership of the political process, which they identify with the machinery of the State and governance, and they manage this apparatus as if it were separate from and only tenuously connected to the people considered as free and equal citizens, having primacy in the Republic. In effect, a political class has seized power, and the bulk of the citizens feel almost entirely alienated from the political process, narrowly and reductively redefined as the management of state business. One might of course also say that this is a two-way process, since it is also arguable that the bulk of the citizens have excluded themselves from the business of politics, pursuing only narrow sectional interests when they engage with politics at all, with the result that on the one hand there is a paralysing resentment at being governed but not heard, and on the other side an impatience with a citizenry that won't just butt out and leave the adults to run the business. Both attitudes are toxic, of course, and the end result is both a dysfunctional citizenry and a state grown increasingly shrill and defensive in proclaiming its legitimacy.

Leaving aside the peculiar way in which the Constitutional Convention has been set up, the secretiveness surrounding the 'public' nominees, the frankly uninspiring line-up of professional politicians named to the process and the suspicion that the government fully intends to ignore any recommendations it doesn't care for, I am left with a great sense of unease that we are merely tinkering with the foundational document of the State when we would be much better employed in taking a long hard look at that same document, and asking ourselves whether, in whole or in parts, it is fit for purpose.

In many ways, the 1937 Constitution was a progressive document in the context of its time, and there is much that is good in it. There is, of course, much that is not, but time and the Supreme Court have gone some way towards ameliorating some of what seems to us now either malign in its intent and effect or merely silly in its outmoded aspirational perspectives.

A great deal has changed in the social and political identity of the Irish people in the intervening years, most notably in our concepts of equality, equity and social justice, and there is unmistakably a case for revising elements of the document in this light, in some cases so severely as to effectively rewrite those provisions in their entirety. What might be the most radical change in our polity since the promulgation of the Constitution, however, came about a mere twelve years after it saw the light of day.

In 1949, almost offhandedly, we declared our State a republic. Remarkably, nobody seems to have thought that this should have prompted a long, cold, hard look at the Constitution. I say remarkably, because the Constitution we still have was not then and is not still in any meaningful sense the constitution of a republic.

Clearly, and this is an attitude with long, tangled roots, we thought that simply to call ourselves a republic was sufficient warrant to think ourselves a republic, as if the act of naming alone would suffice, without further thought, to bring a republic into being.

In some of the essays contained in this book you will find learned and thoughtful consideration of what, in fact, a republic means. Drawing on historical propositions, on philosophical definitions, on precedents of existing or disappeared self-proclaimed republics, different authors offer a wide range of perspectives on what we might mean by the term 'republic.' It is significant, I think, that neither the government of the time, the framers of the Constitution nor any political party since then has been much concerned to engage with such a fundamental discussion.

My own strong instinct finds a pithy expression in Connolly's famous formula: 'Ireland without her people means nothing to me.' It seems to me that the constitution of a republic, considered as a collective agreement between ourselves, requires that first and foremost we consider what it is that binds us as citizens in a common compact, before ever we turn to consider the nature and remit of the concomitant necessary state.

We never did that.

There was not then, nor has there been since, a thoroughgoing debate, concentrated or dispersed, aimed at discovering how it was we meant to constitute ourselves as a body politic with the aim of advancing the common good. There was never a broad, all-encompassing debate aimed not at the essentialist question, 'what is the Irish nation?' but at the more practical, urgent and productive question, 'who do we intend, acting in concert, to be?' We never asked ourselves, 'how do we mean to encompass by agreement the mutual and sometimes conflicting best interests of men and women, of city and country, of the poor, the middling and the rich?' We never asked ourselves, 'how do we propose to provide for the maximum of individual liberty, while recognising that limits will necessarily be set on that liberty by a concern for the common social good?' We never thought to enshrine in perpetuity the fundamental principles of equality, solidarity and justice for all in a state whose sole *raison d'être* would be or should be to provide a framework in which these values would take root and flourish.

Without these debates, it is difficult for me to conceive of how we could proclaim ourselves a republic, a democratic political entity enshrining and constantly giving new impetus to our life in common as citizens, in the light of a perpetually evolving history.

One of my hopes for this book is that it might make a contribution towards a thoroughgoing discussion of what we intend and mean when we say that we are a republic. Another is that we might begin to consider how ambitious, how broad in its scope, a constitution should be, especially in its aspect of giving shelter to our best vision of ourselves as that vision evolves.

Without such discussion, aimed at establishing a firm philosophical base for what we mean when we call ourselves a republic, the term will remain opaque, insubstantial and of little practical use in our ongoing politics. Perhaps the worst consequence of neglecting this philosophical inquiry is that it has allowed the lazy conflation of 'Republican' with 'Nationalist' to persist – and we have seen to our cost the damage this has caused. I should hope that it goes without saying that a broader, more generous idea of the Republic is possible, one that embraces difference, a rational and desirable definition of a better way to organise and provide for justice, prosperity and equity.

I do not intend here to summarise or indeed pre-empt the arguments advanced in the book by its distinguished contributors. Nor do I intend to make use of the book to recruit them in support of an argument of my own. With the exception of Orla O'Connor, the other authors here offer us revised versions of the talks they gave at the 2012 Douglas Hyde Conference. I regret that due to pressure of time it was not possible to invite Ms O'Connor to participate in the conference itself, but I am glad to publish her paper here in what we might best consider a colloquy, a conversation aimed at the sharing of insights and exploring the possibility of a constructive consensus. In truth, I invited our original authors to contribute to the conference because I hoped myself to encounter fresh, learned and provocative perspectives on this most important topic. I hoped better to educate myself, and to share that education with fellow citizens in an open forum. In none of this was I disappointed.

There is much said here with which I agree, much with which I disagree or partially disagree; certainly not all of the authors agree with each other, and at least one would certainly disagree with my jaundiced view of the Constitutional Convention. This, I think, is all to the good. My wish here is not to advocate a premature conclusion, but to help clear the ground and, if I can, help advance discussion to a point where we can maturely ask: 'very well then, what is to be done?'

Not talk for talk's sake, then, but robust discussion that may, if we are fortunate, provoke and inspire us to what I devoutly believe we need: a genuine and sincere impetus towards a Constitution appropriate to who we have become in the long decades since 1937, however we may ultimately decide to frame that charter or document, whether the way leads to reform and restatement or to something wholly new.

2.

It is not just Ireland that has changed in those long, turbulent decades since 1937, the whole world has changed; new ways of thinking have emerged, new perspectives on what it is to be human, new thought, above all, on our common stewardship of our native planet home. In the decades to come, it will not be enough to construct a new Constitution for Ireland in a hermetically sealed vacuum. We will need to consider our polity in the larger context of the European Union, in the context of our privileged membership in the club of developed countries and in the wider context of our responsibilities and our sense of ourselves in the wider human family.

We will also have to consider, as a matter of increasing urgency, how justice, equality and solidarity are not only in need of definition and understanding, but also require active sharing with all the other polities on our beleaguered planet.

We need, above all, the courage of imagination, the nerve and verve to think differently. And, certainly, the humility and intelligence to look beyond our habitual frames of reference for inspiration.

As a spur to this, perhaps, I draw the reader's attention to the wholly new Constitution adopted by Ecuador in 2008, following a comprehensive process that took no more than seven months. The Ecuadorean Constitutional Convention was charged with producing a wholly new document in that time frame, and succeeded in producing a Constitution that is exact and severe in its formulation, while being both exhilarating, wide-ranging and, in many of its aspects, startlingly progressive.

As an example of the scope and ambition of this new Constitution, I will cite the following Articles:

Article 281 reads: 'Food sovereignty is a strategic objective and an obligation of the State in order to ensure that persons, communities, peoples and nations achieve self-sufficiency with respect to healthy and culturally appropriate food on a permanent basis.'

Among the obligations assumed by the State under this section are: 'Strengthen the development of organizations and networks of producers and consumers and the commercialization and distribution of food to promote equity within rural and urban spaces.'

As well as:

'Generate just and solidarity [oriented] systems of distribution and commercialization of food. Impede monopolistic practices and any type of speculation with food products.'

Consider the implications of a like Article in a future Irish Constitution.

Even more radically, Articles 71-74 of the new Constitution confer rights on the natural environment, what we might term 'ecosystem rights', and situates the human holistically inside an eco-political system that is both moral and intensely matter-of-fact:

Article 71. 'Nature, or Pacha Mama, where life is reproduced and occurs, has the right to integral respect for its existence and for the maintenance and regeneration of its life cycles, structure, functions and evolutionary processes.

All persons, communities, peoples and nations can call upon public authorities to enforce the rights of nature. To enforce and interpret these rights, the principles set forth in the Constitution shall be observed, as appropriate.

The State shall give incentives to natural persons and legal entities and to communities to protect nature and to promote respect for all the elements comprising an ecosystem.'

Article 72. 'Nature has the right to be restored. This restoration shall be apart from the obligation of the State and natural persons or legal entities to compensate individuals and communities that depend on affected natural systems.

In those cases of severe or permanent environmental impact, including those caused by the exploitation of nonrenewable natural resources, the State shall establish the most effective mechanisms to achieve the restoration and shall adopt adequate measures to eliminate or mitigate harmful environmental consequences.'

Article 73. 'The State shall apply preventive and restrictive measures on activities that might lead to the extinction of species, the destruction of ecosystems and the permanent alteration of natural cycles.

The introduction of organisms and organic and inorganic material that might definitively alter the nation's genetic assets is forbidden.'

Article 74. 'Persons, communities, peoples and nations shall have the right to benefit from the environment and the natural wealth enabling them to enjoy the good way of living.

Environmental services shall not be subject to appropriation; their production, delivery, use and development shall be regulated by the State.'

My final example:

Article 11.

'The exercise of rights shall be governed by the following principles: 1. Rights can be exercised, promoted and enforced individually or collectively before competent authorities; these authorities shall guarantee their enforcement. 2. All persons are equal and shall enjoy the same rights, duties and opportunities. No one shall be discriminated against for reasons of ethnic belonging, place of birth, age, sex, gender identity, cultural identity, civil status, language, religion, ideology, political affiliation, legal record, socio-economic condition, migratory status, sexual orientation, health status, HIV carrier, disability, physical difference or any other distinguishing feature, whether personal or collective, temporary or permanent, which might be aimed at or result in the diminishment or annulment of recognition, enjoyment or exercise of rights. All forms of discrimination are punishable by law. The State shall adopt affirmative action measures that promote real equality for the benefit of the rights-bearers who are in a situation of inequality.'

We are accustomed, if we think about the matter at all, to refer our own Constitution, vaguely, to the American and French eighteenth-century precedents. There are, of course, more pertinent twentieth-century precedents to consider also, as Gerard Hogan, among others, has pointed out. None of these precedents, it seems to me, are as thoroughgoing, as ambitious in their scope or as exhilarating in their vision of what it is to be fully human as this present Ecuadorean model. I offer these examples here, and encourage the reader to read the entire thing for herself or himself, as a spur and incentive to imagination.

3.

I began by making reference to the sense most citizens have now of being powerless and disenfranchised except in the most rudimentary sense of enfranchisement. I believe that this is a very dangerous state of affairs. Equally dangerous is our current system of government, which at the present moment consists, in its active component, of two elements: the so-called Troika, which issues its instructions to the Cabinet, and the Gang of Four, the ruling cabal in the Cabinet, which determines how these instructions are to be implemented. There is now no sense at all in which any government TD is fully carrying out his or her role as a Teachta Dála, a legate or delegate to the Dáil, empowered and authorised to convey to the Parliament the instructions, wishes, hopes and aspirations of her or his constituency. Government TDs now, whatever their individual views and qualities, are permitted to be and act as little more than automatons whose sole function is to acquiesce in the decisions of the Cabinet – which means, instrumentally, the decisions of the Gang of Four at the behest of the Troika.

I believe that nothing can now bridge the chasm between State and citizen except a complete restatement of the compact that binds us together in common cause. We must find it in ourselves to frame new words that will bind up our hearts, hands and minds in a new ambition for ourselves; we need to find it in ourselves to set aside pettiness, a defect in our hopes, a cruel narrowing in the scope of our dreaming. We need to constitute ourselves again.

The Politics of the Constitutional Convention

Maura Adshead

Introduction: Why Politics Matters

Without ever really thinking about it, we all know what politics is. It is a necessary evil. Something that we intuitively do not like, but know that we must have. It is politics that runs the State, keeps the government in power and provides for the people. Most of us feel that the State could be better run, the government could be better managed and that the people could be better provided for. Yet we do not rebel. Deep down, we understand that it is not an easy job. Yet still we find it distasteful. Deep down, we are sceptical that those in politics really do care about us. It is, after all, a strangely altruistic and thankless sort of job. Not the kind of job that normal people might do. But, nevertheless, one that must be done.

In fact, politics is an activity that is central to the practice of democracy. The truth is, although we like to pretend that it is otherwise, mass democracy – in terms of the vote being available to all adults – is an incredibly recent phenomenon. I still remember my mother telling me that it was a privilege for which people died. And that is why we should cherish it. Because, despite our current economic woes, it is a system that enables us to provide standards in health, welfare, housing, education and employment that are unattainable in any other system. According to the IMF, in the birthplace of democracy, at the end of 2011, after four years of recession, Greece still had a higher GDP per capita, based on purchasing power parity (PPP), than any other country in South America and Africa as well as most of Asia.[1] None of the much-touted BRICs (Brazil, Russia, India, China, South Africa) has a GDP per capita even close to the European 'sick man'. And central to this system is the practice of good politics. Good politics delivers the opportunity to listen to others, the opportunity to engage in dialogue, the opportunity to compromise, and to do deals. These are all absolutely central to any democratic process.

In Ireland, a country famed for 'the gift of the gab' and our capacity to 'deal with the devil', we have perhaps grown complacent about the possibilities that good politics provides for our economic and social well-being. We have become fixed in the view that nothing ever really changes, and no real change can be achieved. Indeed, according to an *Irish Times* editorial, 'it is striking how little political debate or wider public discourse there has been about what Ireland we should strive for after this economic crisis.'[2] It seems, for the moment at least, that we have lost belief in our capacity to change things for the better. Why is this the case? One reason is that we have lost confidence in our politicians. The other reason is that we have lost confidence in ourselves.

A Crisis of Confidence in Our Politicians

Politics is probably the only career in the world where professional practitioners do not sue or get sued when they are accused, or when they accuse someone else, of doing their job badly. This is an odd sort of a profession. Can you imagine doctors carrying on like this?

Imagine if you hurt your leg and were left with a large bruise. You might wonder if you should call the doctor for advice, or maybe a physiotherapist. What would you do if you called the doctor and she said, 'Whatever you do don't go to the physiotherapist – he knows nothing, he's deceitful and his approach is all wrong.' You're not sure if she's right, so you ring the physiotherapist, who tells you, 'Pay no attention to that doctor. I've been saying for years that she doesn't know what she's doing. The situation with your leg is very unfortunate, but you're best off letting me look after it.'

Which one would you trust? Fortunately for those of us with sore legs, it is widely recognised that this is not a professional way to behave. At the end of the day, even if two leg specialists have their differences, a professional code of conduct ensures that they do not cause unnecessary confusion and anxiety to would-be patients. A professional code of conduct means that they can simply explain how their treatment works, how it differs to other kinds of treatment and what the likely benefits and side effects might be. To do otherwise would be daft: if doctors and physiotherapists carried on bad-mouthing each other like that, in the end the real losers would be the patients, who would get so cynical and confused that they would trust neither, stop going to either, and end up with no relief at all. That carry on would be mad. No business could work that way. Except one.

In the operation of politics, discrediting the opposition is a fairly routine part of doing business. And whereas in other professions there are regulatory associations setting standards of office, in politics the poacher has turned gamekeeper and politicians themselves set the standards for public office. The best guarantee for democracy, we are usually told, is freedom of the press. Yet as the media has changed, so too has its role. The internet, Facebook and Twitter have revolutionised traditional print media: many people now get their news through their own selected network of friends and web pages. The capacity that the traditional press once had to lead a story or shape it is consequently diminished. The interactivity of tweeting on a trending article means that our broadcasters and journalists are as much responding to us as we are to them. So now, not alone do we have a bunch of professional politicians all giving out about each other, but those who stand in judgment over them are just as keen to join the fray. Is this a sensible way to censure a profession? Can you imagine watching a science programme where the journalist constantly asked the scientist investigating a cure for cancer: 'So why haven't you done this yet? You've been looking at this problem for years, what's wrong with you?' That is the tone of the conversation we get with almost all politicians, yet the complexity of the administrative, political and economic systems that they are trying to influence and change is enormous. In this climate of opinion, are we really sure that we are having the most productive discussion about the options for good governance?

A Crisis of Confidence in Ourselves

Although we are routinely accused of increasing apathy, in fact there are not dramatically fewer people interested in politics than was ever the case. Politics has always attracted a few keen enthusiasts, with a much larger range of ordinary citizens who feel that they would like to be acknowledged or heard, but have no keen interest in political participation themselves. What perhaps has changed is the feeling of this larger majority that their opinions and concerns are being acknowledged: for many, the sense that the ordinary majority matters is in decline. In other words, people's sense of belief and trust in the system is wavering.

There are a variety of reasons for this. One is that as citizens of the most well-off liberal democracies in the world, we have grown used to a life free from war, want and repression. We enjoy higher standards of living, income, education and attainment than ever before, and in consequence we now have more facilities, time and resources to nurture aspirations and desires that many citizens in less well-off parts of the world have no time to even dream of. This view of society, characterised by Inglehart[3] as the post-materialist thesis, suggests that it is our very success that breeds new and unfulfilled political aspirations and desires. But there are other reasons also.

Rapid globalisation in the last few decades has, for many, generated a sense of powerlessness in the face of rapid social change. Whilst for some it is the engine of modernisation and economic growth, for others it portends the triumph of economics over politics, exposing us to hard competition, driving down wages at the bottom and driving up rewards at the top, an inescapable tide of inequality moving across the world. In fact, with good politics it need not be either, but more often than not globalisation provides a useful cover for indecision and fear: it does not automatically drive wealth and power towards inequality, but it does sow enough confusion and uncertainty to make decisive action look like too much trouble. According to Runciman,[4] modern democracy is a confused and confusing business, and it takes a lot of time and trouble to find your way through it. The people who are running the show seem as confused as anyone about how we got here. They didn't mean it to turn out like this, and they would quite like to do something about it. They just don't know how. The funny thing is that he's not talking about Ireland at all. The point is that he may just as well be.

Both these developments together combine to feed the last significant cause of our current crisis in confidence: in the last few years, the nature of political engagement has changed dramatically. In the post-war world of forty or fifty years ago, political parties and trade unions were effective tools – not only to aggregate political preferences and set political agendas, but to breed a sense of common solidarity and common interest amongst groups of citizens. Both are now in decline. In their stead, it is suggested that social networks and 'virtual communities' can provide the same political function.[5] But is this really the case? In 2010, Malcolm Gladwell was widely criticised for an article he wrote in the *New Yorker*, which disputed the far-reaching political effects of social networking.[6] In 2011, the Arab Spring and Occupy Wall Street movements posed a challenge to this point of view. The benefit of hindsight, however, suggests that the argument is not so clear-cut. There is much to suggest that a 'networked, weak-tie world' will be trumped by the strong ties of personal relationships built on shared first-hand experiences, whether in government or amongst its opponents.[7] It is this element of personalism that has routinely been noted as a prominent feature of Irish politics.[8] The problem, it seems then, is that though Irish politics has maintained a strong element of personalism and localism in its political expression, we seem somewhere to have lost the ability to join together and put our views across in coherent collective political expression. Individually, we can lobby for planning permission – but as a collective we seem incapable of expressing a clear view on the need for planning restrictions and laws. Individually, we can complain about the quality of our water supply – but as a collective we seem incapable of adhering to a collective view on environmental regulation. In short, the crisis of confidence that we have in our power to influence the political realm arises primarily as a consequence of the inefficacy of our political engagement.

The remainder of this chapter gives a brief review of our history of attempts at collective political engagement in Ireland, the forms that it has taken and the lessons that can be learned, and perhaps applied to the most recent foray into political engagement: the Constitutional Convention.

Political Engagement in Ireland – A Whirlwind Tour

That Ireland fought for independence and then entered directly into civil war to contest the outcome certainly demonstrates that not too long ago Irish people felt politically engaged to the extent that they would take up arms to defend their political preferences. Since the foundation of the Republic, we have been less inclined towards such extreme forms of political engagement, and it is quite probably precisely because of our close experience with civil war on such a small and intimate scale that we have tended wherever possible to work towards a consensus. Nevertheless, the political institutions that were established in the Republic provided a range of mechanisms for political engagement. The first and most conspicuous of these are the variety of means by which we may directly express our opinion by voting. These include general and local elections, presidential elections and referenda. The second are a series of formal and semi-formal quasi-corporatist institutional arrangements for representation, including the Seanad, the NESC, Social Partnership and the NESF. Third, there are those social movements directly set up by, or designed to facilitate the representation of, mass citizen engagement with the government. These include, but are not limited to, the 'Claiming our Future', 'Second Republic' and We the Citizens' campaigns.

Political Engagement via a Vote

Notwithstanding our ability to vote in local and presidential elections, when most of us think of elections, we tend to think of the general elections used to determine our government. By law, a general election to the Dáil must be held at least once every five years. There are 166

Teachtaí Dála (TDs or members of the Dáil), representing the forty-one electoral constituencies into which the State is divided. No constituency may return fewer than three members, and larger constituencies may be represented by up to five TDs. Since, however, the primary focus of PR STV is on the choice of individual representatives, in the Republic of Ireland there is an obvious resonance with the old cliché that 'all politics is local.' Ireland's single transferable vote (STV) method of proportional representation (PR), which allows voters to mark as many preferences as there are candidates in multiple-seat constituencies, not only obliges candidates of the same party to compete against each other, but also offers the opportunity for voters to switch between parties, according to their preferences. The result is a highly personalised and localised electoral competition, where issues of national policy often take second place (or may be considered equally important) to issues of local concern.

Just as significant is the way in which the electoral system tends to refract national policy issues into local politics. Thus, for example, in the election of 2002, most of the fourteen independent seats went to those candidates 'characteristically arguing that the constituency, or even one part of it, had not received its fair share of government spending.'[9] Three had distinctive health-related platforms, and one argued for a better share of infrastructural investment for her constituency.[10] In another electoral system, hospital closures and specialised care, as well as national infrastructure, might be considered issues of national policy rather than issues of specific local concern. Moreover, it could be argued that by allowing local constituencies to vent their concerns via the election of independents, the larger parties were able to treat these as local issues and avoid making them the subject of national political debate.

This need not be the case. In the 2007 election, the Fine Gael/Labour coalition of opposition against the incumbent Fianna Fáil/Progressive Democrat Government made health one of their primary campaign issues.[11] The point is that in the PR-STV electoral system, political parties may choose whether to contest the election on local or national issues. This is a dysfunctional trend in Irish elections: the more concerned we are about political issues, the greater is our propensity to vote for independent candidates whom we believe can represent our concerns. In the 2011 Election, the number of candidates running as independents for smaller parties (registered as 'other' to the established political parties) was 233, compared to the 108 in 2007.[12] It reflects once more the difficulty that the Irish political system has in articulating a common political concern. This is because, in reality, when independent candidates provide a lightning rod for important citizen concerns they effectively channel voter frustration away from the mainstream parties, and enable the major parties to remove that issue from their priority list. Worse again, in a deal to make up the numbers to govern, the major parties may accede to independent demands and the common resources of the country will be divided out in a way that secures a political bargain rather than one that maximises value for money or fairness in service provision to the majority.

The pre-eminence of localism engendered by our electoral system makes the constituency work of TDs disproportionately burdensome, leading Farrell[13] to note an 'evident consensus among deputies that the competition in constituency service has got out of hand' – a point that has been confirmed by a number of politicians from a variety of political parties since.[14] At national level, the emphasis on the local constituency work arguably detracts politicians from focusing on national political issues. Local constituency work is not only extremely time-consuming, but its significance serves to diminish the importance of other TD roles. Writing in the *Sunday Independent*, TD for Limerick East Willie O'Dea candidly noted that 'backbenchers spend 80% of their time servicing individual constituents – to the detriment of the national interest.'[15] As a result of this, he argued, 'the garnering of a few dozen medical cards is more vital to political survival than any creative well-researched Dáil speech on health service reform.'[16] As it stands, however, we cannot criticise our TDs for behaving like this: they are responding to the logic of our system. I can think of no other reason why the Minister for Finance, in the midst of complex rounds of diplomacy on IMF/EU bailout plans and promissory notes, should find it necessary to take time out to officially open a bookstore in Limerick.[17]

Within this context, the local constituency skills needed to be a successful politician in Ireland may not be the most desirable in terms of national politics. In their attempts to achieve electoral popularity, Irish politicians may tend to follow public opinion rather than lead it. It is argued that this leads to a notable level of 'cautiousness' amongst our politicians that has a significant impact on policy outcomes.[18] In Irish politics, it is often the case that where public opinion is most divided, politicians will be most reticent in advancing their own opinions. Perhaps the most conspicuous example of this is the unwillingness of Irish governments (or legislature) to put forward legislation on abortion.[19] It was not until a pregnant woman was denied a termination and subsequently died in hospital[20] that public outrage was sufficient to move the government to address this issue.[21] The system conspires, however, to make a referendum a more attractive option.[22]

Extensive recourse to direct democracy to settle key political issues in the Republic is a unique feature of Irish politics. Since 1937, there have been more than thirty referenda on issues including the electoral system (1959, 1968); initial entry into the European Community (1972) and subsequent EU treaty revisions (1987, 1992, 2001); the position of the State on 'moral' issues such as the special position of the Catholic Church (1972), abortion within the State (1983), access to abortion information and services outside the State (1992), divorce (1986, 1995); access to bail (1997); removal of the death penalty (2001); legislative provisions for constitutionally permitted abortion in Ireland (2002), the Nice Treaty (2002); citizenship (2004); the Lisbon Treaty (2008 and again in 2009); judges' remuneration and Oireachtas committees (2011); EU/IMF bailout conditions (2012) and children's rights (2012).

In terms of a referendum's capacity to provide for political engagement, however, referenda are a very blunt instrument to decipher the common interest.[23] Notwithstanding the scepticism of some academics and politicians, most ordinary Irish people are extremely fond of our electoral system and its proclivity for referenda. To my mind, it is another example of our dysfunctional political engagement. There are very few politically complex issues can be adequately dealt with by a yes or no answer. We cannot have referenda on complicated questions of policy without a necessary dumbing down of the debate or a reframing of the debate in a way that facilitates a simple aggregation of yes or no answers. If our history is anything to go by, the three contested referenda on abortion that we have already had, in 1983, 1992 and 2002, suggest that a fourth will not provide an adequate answer to such a complex and divisive issue. In terms of political engagement, it seems that for some things a vote is not the answer: some political issues need a more thoughtful discussion.

And central to this is the practice of good politics. Good politics delivers the opportunity to listen to others, the opportunity for dialogue, and the opportunity to compromise, so that as many people as possible are as happy as is practicable with a jointly authored solution.

So if voting is not always the answer, what other fora do we have to facilitate political engagement?

Political Engagement via an Institution

When de Valera redrafted the 1937 Constitution, it is no secret that he was influenced by the corporatist ideals espoused by contemporary Jesuit scholars, and ever since it has been possible to discern the principles of Catholic social teaching in the corporatist tendencies of a range of Irish representative institutions. Whilst the Catholic Church approved of private property and the capitalist system, it disapproved of competitive individualism: it did not rate the idea of Marxist class conflict at all! According to the Church, in a well-ordered society individual greed should be curbed, and the authorities should ensure a fair distribution of income. The various occupational groups should feel themselves part of a greater whole, linked by feelings of social responsibility, rather than divided into social classes. This attitudinal proclivity in our political culture is evidenced in a range of significant attempts to develop political participation via formal and semi-formal institutions constituted outside of direct democracy and universal balloting.

The first and most conspicuous example is de Valera's design for Seanad Éireann, which was intentionally vocationalist, representing the key strands of Irish economic, political and cultural life. In addition to the eleven senators nominated by the Taoiseach and the six elected by a selection of universities, forty-three are elected from five panels: cultural and educational; agricultural; labour; industrial and commercial; and administrative. Although this idea was seeded into the Seanad's terms of reference from the outset, in practice the significance of party politics soon outweighed the significance of any collective interest within the panels. In 2004, the *Report on Seanad Reform* argued that 'its arcane and outdated system of nomination and election diminishes Senators' legitimacy' and creates a situation whereby 'unless a candidate comes from a political background, he/she has practically no chance of getting elected.'[24] In short, the political design intended to represent collective and common interests did not follow its design features: instead, party politics trumped collective interests.

Another – perhaps less well-known but more influential – attempt at quasi-corporatist political engagement is evidenced in the establishment of the National Economic and Social Committee (NESC). The NESC was established in 1973 under the aegis of the Department of the Taoiseach and tasked with providing advice to the government on the development of the national economy and the achievement of social justice. The Council of NESC is intended to reflect the major economic and social interests in society. Until 1998, when community and voluntary sector representatives joined, the NESC was composed of key Government department representatives, the trade unions, business and employer organisations, and agricultural and farming organisations. The NESC is credited by the government, business and unions as the most important institutional progenitor for the system of national social partnership that dominated Irish policy making for two decades until its collapse in 2008/9.

On the one hand, the NESC has been described by *The Irish Times*[25] as 'the alternative Parliament,' diminishing even further the authority of the Dáil. Ward[26] notes that from 1987, 'the National Economic and Social Council prepared reports for the government, without reference to the Oireachtas or political parties, which amounted to national plans for economic and tax policy, social reform, welfare, health, education, and much more.' When both Fine Gael and Labour complained of their exclusion from the process, 'they were told by the government that there would have been no agreement on the NESC's plan if parties had been involved.'[27]

On the other hand, it is argued that during the 1980s the NESC provided the social partners with a neutral space for frank and robust discussions. Those who were present remember 'a huge level of blame and also a high level of mistrust' between the participants.[28] Nevertheless, it provided a 'place where the key people met, even if they were continuously disagreeing',[29] and the conventions of confidentiality at NESC meetings enabled them to express their views candidly, not so much as public representatives for their organisations, but more as leaders and managers who had a keen sense of what was and was not organisationally possible.[30] It is suggested that 'Even though the [NESC] reports were not of any use, from the point of view of trying to implement them, it was really out of that process that a willingness to attempt a common resolution was framed.'[31] In short, the NESC provided a 'safe space' for discussions that eventually went beyond posturing to negotiating. The increasing importance of the NESC as the 'engine of partnership' is well recognised by all of the social partners, so much so that many of them refer to participation in the NESC as the partnership 'process'.[32]

Through this system a number of institutional developments evolved, under the aegis of the Department of the Taoiseach, providing for a complex web of working groups and committees to analyse and address specific policy problems.[33] It is certainly doubtful whether anyone involved in this system of policy-making initially intended or conceived of it as a new way of governing, but over time this kind of consultative policy-making became a well-established *modus vivendi*, and 'government by partnership' became strongly embedded as the cornerstone of Irish governance.[34] By the mid 1990s, all of the main political parties had been involved at one stage or another of the partnership process, and business and union representatives began to acknowledge 'the cultural shift' to partnership governance.[35] From the government's point of view, there was an acknowledgement of the collective comfort in those peak-level engagements that people brought to the table.[36] In the words of one seasoned social partner: 'We have established ways of solving problems ... And it's always resolved sitting around a table, it's not resolved from people marching or people going on strike or taking extreme positions or whatever.'[37] While recognising the benefits of such norms, however, others have wondered whether or not they bring with them the potential for stagnation.[38]

In 1997, the inclusion of the community and voluntary pillar in the social partnership arrangements reflected the government's acknowledgement of the importance of civil society in public policy deliberations.[39] This point had already been conceded by the Fianna Fáil/Labour coalition government with the creation of the National Economic and Social Forum (NESF) in 1993. Set up under the Office of the Tánaiste, which was itself an innovation demanded by Labour's inclusion in the coalition, the NESF was 'designed to include women's organisations, the unemployed, the disadvantaged, youth, the elderly and people with a disability, in order that they might influence public policy.'[40] For some, the inclusion of the community and voluntary pillar into social partnership arrangements represented a 'squaring of the circle', so that all important elements of society were now engaged in the process; for others, it sowed the seeds of its decline, by bringing more diverse interests into well-established processes of negotiation. By the time of their inclusion, however, 'government by partnership' was assumed to be a panacea for all kinds of policy problems, one that could be applied to much broader policy issues such as strengthening local democracy and tackling social exclusion, as well as fostering local development and achieving economic growth. This assumption not only increased the complexity of the set of policy problems that partnership approach was required to address, but also changed the terms used to evaluate its success. That partnership approaches were sometimes found wanting as a consequence was in some respects inevitable.

It is in this context that the NESF reflected a deliberate attempt by the government to engage directly with the marginalised and disadvantaged in society, and it was to play a key role in the next government's National Anti-Poverty Strategy (NAPS), which lasted from 1997 to 2007. The NESF, which already had responsibility for monitoring the social inclusion element of the national agreement 1997–2000, Partnership 2000, was asked to report specifically on the progress of the NAPS implementation. The Combat Poverty Agency was charged with overseeing the evaluation of the NAPS process, 'which would include consideration of the views and experience of the community and voluntary sector,' and report back to the government's co-ordinating committee.[41] In July 2009, the Combat Poverty Agency, which had been in existence since 1986, was 'integrated' into the Office for Social Inclusion, housed in the Department of Social and Family Affairs until

May 2010, and in the Department of Community, Equality and Gaeltacht Affairs thereafter. In April 2010, the NESF (together with the National Centre for Partnership and Performance) was dissolved, and its core functions integrated back into the NESC. The NESC Council was asked to adapt its work programme to ensure that appropriate aspects of the work of the NESF would be continued.

In her statement on the dissolution of the NESF, its chair Dr Maureen Gaffney formally recorded that the NESF 'was the first social partnership body that included not just the traditional social partners, but representatives from the voluntary and community sector,' as well as being 'the only social partnership body with representatives from the Oireachtas, whose wide-ranging experience of policy-making and emerging issues also greatly enriched the work of the Forum.'[42] The Taoiseach, Enda Kenny, explained that the decision arose out of consideration of a value-for-money review carried out by his Department and also the special review group on public service numbers and expenditure programmes.[43] He used the same rationale to propose a referendum on the abolition of the Seanad, promising 'to take a hands-on role in campaigning for its abolition.'[44]

All in all, though there are clearly mixed views about the performance and democratic shortcomings of institutionalised partnership arrangements, the fact that they were created in the first place suggests that they represented an attempt to address some perceived political deficit. Those who participated typically refer to the opportunities that they afforded for consultation and relationship building. When interviewed, participants in social partnership referred not only to the direct benefits of negotiations, but to more indirect benefits that are seen as accruing from these informal processes, such as 'increasing the capacity of senior civil servants'[45] or advancing the ability to 'influence by osmosis.'[46] Others considered that 'The real win is actual influence and the participative process whereby you are very close to the centre in terms of what is happening.'[47]

Over and again, participants referred to the opportunity to listen to others, the opportunity for dialogue, the opportunity to compromise and to do deals. Whatever the shortcomings of the particular institutions discussed here, more generally, providing some institutional space for this kind of activity is absolutely central to democratic politics. Notwithstanding the continued existence of the NESC, it seems that in the contemporary political climate we are in danger of concluding that we neither need nor can afford such a luxury in Irish politics. Still our various attempts to create institutional fora for political engagement – from the Seanad, to the NESF and the complex systems underpinning social partnership – point to an enduring desire for political engagement; perhaps one that is not always satisfied, but a desire that persists nevertheless.

So if political engagement via institutions is not always the answer, what other fora do we have to facilitate political engagement?

Political Engagement via People Power

In the Republic of Ireland, civic activism takes place via a wide range of organisations, covering every area of social, cultural and economic life. The sub-sector that has seen the greatest growth in recent years is that concerned with ethnic minorities, refugees and asylum seekers – a sub-group that itself makes up a significant proportion of volunteers across a range of voluntary groups (perhaps a partial result of the under-employment of some ethnic minorities and non-eligibility for work of asylum seekers). Taking all voluntarist sectors together, 'Ireland shows higher levels of engagement in informal social networks and community activism than the UK, higher rates of involvement in membership organisations, and a greater confidence that ordinary people can make a difference to public decision making.'[48] Are we generating more heat than light? For all of our altruism and voluntary activity, we still seem convinced that we cannot change our politics. In 2010, one eminent political scientist considered Irish civil society as 'stagnant and passive.'[49] The problem, according to Murphy,[50] is that despite the range of voluntary and community interests, they have historically been shaped into 'silos' or discrete sectors (women, disability, unions, environment, farming, etc.), which have nursed their own interests above those of the collective. It is argued that this tendency was further reinforced by partnership approaches, making it much less likely for sectional interests to become engaged in broader macro-policy debate.[51] Nevertheless, in the last year or two, at least three substantive 'people power' movements have emerged to contest this established view.

Claiming our Future

Claiming our Future is 'a progressive movement for an equal, sustainable and thriving Ireland.' The movement emerged following a series of meetings between the Irish Congress of Trade Unions, environmental groups, the Community Platform, Social Justice Ireland and TASC (Think tank for Action on Social Change) about how best to co-operate and co-ordinate endeavours for a more equal, inclusive and sustainable Ireland. Through a series of seminars, workshops, public campaigns, media events and other forms of publicity, the movement is designed to bring greater visibility to the range of civil society organisations and advocacy groups who are keen to explore and share alternative options to those currently favoured in the dominant economic paradigm. Key policy themes and action agendas relate to issues of equality, environmental sustainability, active participation, governmental accountability, political reform and social solidarity.

The movement began – through the 'Shaping our Future' campaign – as a 'deliberative exercise, talking, listening and building trust with other sectors in Irish progressive civil society.'[52] Over a series of tentative meetings, three key principles emerged: 'that action should be society-led in state-free public spheres; that cross sectoral work was important; and that methods are needed to enable national and local mobilization and deliberation.'[53] Accordingly, on 30 October 2010, a large-scale public deliberative event was held, primed by up to twenty local meetings and twenty national planning activities held throughout the country. 1,300 people registered their attendance, and 100 trained facilitators volunteered their time for the event. Extensive use was made of social media, and deliberative dialogue was further facilitated via the movement's website. Whilst the movement has struggled to capture the same levels of enthusiasm in the longer term, it maintains a relatively healthy infrastructure of groups and networks of support, sending out a monthly e-letter to the 7,000 citizens who have registered on its website. Although routinely mistaken as a front for various left-of-centre organisations and parties, the movement continues to lobby for change and reflects a healthy interest in issues and debates that are seldom raised in more mainstream political settings.

Second Republic

Second Republic is a grass-roots movement for political reform in Ireland, created by a network of ordinary people who believe that 'reform should not be decided by politicians or expert groups in isolation. It needs to be citizen led.' The group began when one of its founding members wrote a letter to *The Irish Times*,[54] inviting anyone interested in joining 'a sustained, serious and credible campaign for wide-ranging political reforms in Ireland' to visit a new discussion forum created for that purpose on the web. The deluge of responses enabled them to convene their first public meeting two weeks later. They subsequently proposed the establishment of a citizens' assembly to deliberate and decide on political reform. Its three key demands, although the Assembly might include politicians or constitutional experts, were that it must: 'have a representative cross-section of Irish people, who will have the final say in its recommendations; make recommendations on reform within twelve months of its formation and have its recommendations put to the people in a referendum within six months of its conclusion.'[55]

Since the beginning of their campaign in 2010, all of the main political parties have adopted policies advocating processes of citizen involvement in the process of reform.

We the Citizens

We the Citizens is, or was, an independent, philanthropically funded initiative, designed to 'explore whether our Republic could benefit by citizens coming together in new ways of public decision-making.' The initiative, spearheaded by a group of academics and public service professionals, hosted seven citizens' events around the country throughout May and June of 2011, in order to provide a space for people to engage with each other on Ireland's future. The views expressed in these events helped to inform the agenda of the 'National Citizens' Assembly', held at the Royal Hospital Kilmainham, and made up from a cross section of one hundred randomly selected Irish people between the ages of 18 and 87. The results of both the Assembly and the meetings that took place prior to it are published in the final report, available from the website.[56]

The report concludes that the initiative provided clear evidence that 'given access to balanced expert information and sufficient time, a randomly selected group of people could make reasoned decisions on important social and political issues.'[57] Hypothesising that by taking part in such an exercise, a randomly selected group of participants could increase their interest and enthusiasm for political engagement, the project asserted that 'after the Citizens' Assembly, participants showed greater interest in politics and also more willingness to discuss and become more involved in politics.'[58] Participants felt more positive about the ability of ordinary people to influence politics. There were in fact large shifts in the opinions of Citizens' Assembly members after they had deliberated on economic issues, such as tax, spending and the sale of public assets. There were also important shifts in the opinions of Citizens' Assembly members regarding the role of TDs, with a clear view emerging that TDs should concentrate more on national legislative and policy work and less on local service.

The full report makes for interesting reading on a number of issues, but what is perhaps most interesting about this study is that it provides robust evidence of statistical significance in the shifts of opinion that arose as a consequence of participating in the Assembly. In layperson's terms, this means that there is clear evidence that the changes in opinions and outcomes from discussion were not a matter of chance, when compared with other random groups who had not participated in the Assembly. It was the process of participating in the Assembly that led to the shift of opinions observed. In other words, it was noted that a randomly selected group of participants in the Assembly had wholeheartedly availed of the opportunity to listen to others, the opportunity for dialogue, the opportunity to compromise, and to do deals on their priorities for political reform. The academics had proven that the political engagement that the Second Republic's ordinary citizens requested, and that the various advocacy organisations associated with Claiming our Future proposed, can occur when we are willing to set up the conditions that support it.

Political Engagement: Exit, Voice or Loyalty?

The options available to most citizens are perhaps best summed up by Hirschman's seminal text, *Exit, Voice and Loyalty*.[59] Now almost a cliché, Hirschman's proposition was that all citizens have essentially two possible responses when they perceive that the organisation or State to which they belong, is exhibiting decreasing quality or benefits to its membership: they can 'exit' and withdraw from the relationship, or they can 'voice' their concerns and attempt to repair or improve the relationship – through communication of their grievances and/or proposal(s) for change. So, for example, workers may choose to leave their unpleasant job, or they may choose to express their concerns in an effort to improve the situation. Essentially, citizens have the same choice: they may emigrate, or they may choose to express their concerns in an effort to improve the situation.

Both these forms of expression – 'exit' and 'voice' – typically reflect a degree of dissatisfaction, but obviously the second is a more useful means of working out exactly what it is that is causing the dissatisfaction. Where greater opportunities exist for 'voice' it is argued that less recourse is taken to 'exit'. Conversely, where the expression of dissatisfaction is stifled, the greater is the temptation to 'exit'. The general principle, therefore, is that the greater the availability of exit, the less likely that voice will be used, but that this relationship can be mediated by the interplay of 'loyalty'. Where group members feel loyalty towards their organisation, or in its political expression where citizens feel loyalty towards the State, the tendency to 'exit' may be reduced and the responsibility to 'voice' may be increased. According to Hirschman, a failure to understand these competing pressures can lead to organisational decline and possible failure.

The parallels between the *Exit, Voice and Loyalty* thesis and the Irish experience of democracy are profound. Generations of Irish emigrants, reaching back long before our current political set-up, have left our political culture with a predisposition for 'exit'. Added to this, our turbulent political experience at the birth of our State, and its impact on our politics thereafter, has engendered within our political culture a reticence for 'voice'. Notwithstanding the strong attachment that most Irish people claim for their country, the loyalty that we feel is seldom expressed in terms of a desire for political engagement. Or at least it wasn't until relatively recently, when we have seen the bubbling up of a new sense of what loyalty to the Republic might actually mean.

Conclusions: Political Engagement via the Constitutional Convention?

Politics is a difficult and unusual business. The stakes are high, and the cost of bad decisions may be felt for generations. In this context, the path of least resistance is tempting indeed – for those charged with making the decisions, for those charged with reporting and investigating those decisions, and for the rest of us choosing which to follow. The rewards of good politics, though, are equally great, and it behoves all of us to ensure that our political system works to the benefit of us all, according to ideals that we are all willing to defend. The Constitutional

Convention provides one such opportunity. It may be limited, it might have been designed differently, it might have been designed better. But are we going to play politics – score points, devalue it and write it off before it has begun? Or are we going to *do* politics? Are we going to take the opportunity to listen to others, the opportunity for dialogue, the opportunity to compromise and to negotiate?

The Constitutional Convention isn't a magic bullet, but it is as good a place as any to start the process of political engagement. In terms of political reform, the Constitutional Convention will not fix much: first because it does not have a broad enough remit; and, second, because most people in Ireland do not want a great deal to change. What the Constitutional Convention does provide is a national platform that could be used for the practice of good politics. Good politics delivers the opportunity to listen to others, the opportunity to dialogue, the opportunity to compromise, and to do deals. These are all absolutely central to any democratic process.

It would be nice if the Constitutional Convention provided a positive experience of political engagement – to let people see that there is something to be learned by the conduct of good politics – and to roundly conclude that this is an activity that we should do regularly and routinely to strengthen and support our democracy.

RECONSTRUCTIVE POTENTIAL IN THE CONSTITUTIONAL CONVENTION

Senator Ivana Bacik

Introduction

As *Bunreacht na hÉireann* has just celebrated its seventy-fifth birthday, it is timely to assess the current status and future direction of the Constitution. It seems especially appropriate to carry out this assessment in the context of a conference celebrating the life of Douglas Hyde, who was elected as president seventy-five years ago this year – and at the commencement of the work of a Constitutional Convention, established to review specific elements of the Constitution that may require amendment.

On one view, however, the Constitution needs no substantial change, as it continues to set out the core principles of the nation's governance, and to ensure the vindication and protection of the fundamental human rights of our citizens.

On an alternative view, the Constitution may be seen as a product of its time, now very much out of date, so much so that radical amendment is necessary in order to ensure its survival for another seven or eight decades.

Some obvious problems with the development of the Constitution may be identified very easily: the growth of the administrative state, or the gap between rhetoric and reality in terms of fundamental rights protection, for example. These flaws are serious enough, and have been dealt with elsewhere, but this paper seeks to focus upon three other features of the Constitution that indicate the need for radical change.

First, the provisions regarding the most fundamental aspects of governance of the State are outdated. Secondly, the Constitution embodies what has been called a 'pro-religion' ethos – particularly apparent in Article 44.1 and the Preamble – committing the courts to a set of constitutional propositions that should not be applied in a republic, or indeed a liberal democracy. The theocratic ideology underlying the text is no longer appropriate or sustainable in modern Ireland, and marks another reason for rewriting.

Thirdly and finally, there is a tension between the theocratic ideology already mentioned, and the somewhat conflicting liberal-democracy ideology that also underlies the fundamental rights provisions. Taken together, these ideologies upon which the Bill of Rights provisions are based are, it is argued, insufficiently cognisant of communitarian principles to fit our contemporary society.

The Status of Republic

The Irish State is legally a republic. But this is not reflected in any provision of the Constitution itself, because in 1937, when the Constitution was adopted, Ireland was not a republic. The Irish Free State was still legally in existence, so reference to any legal basis for the State was studiously avoided in the text. In July 1945, in what became known as the 'Dictionary Republic' speech, Taoiseach Éamon de Valera argued in the Dáil that the Free State was a republic in everything but name. Claiming that this was obvious on the facts, he observed trenchantly: 'The State is what it is, not what I say or think it is. How a particular State is to be classified politically is a matter not to be settled by the *ipse dixit* of any person, but by observation of the State's institutions and an examination of its fundamental laws … look up any standard book of reference and get … any definition of a republic or any description of what a republic is, and judge whether our State does not possess every characteristic mark by which a republic can be distinguished or recognised. We are a democracy with the ultimate sovereign power resting with the people – a representative democracy with the various organs of State functioning under a written Constitution, with the executive authority controlled by Parliament, with an independent judiciary functioning under the Constitution and the law, and with a Head of State directly elected by the people for a definite term of office…'.[60]

Thus the view was taken that the new Constitution created what was to all intents and purposes that of a republic. This view may be contested, however, given the obvious divergence of the Irish State from the secular principles upon which French republicanism is modelled, as evidenced by the theocratic influences obvious in the language of the Preamble and fundamental rights Articles.

De Valera's flexible approach to definitional difficulties might well deserve the description 'an Irish solution to an Irish problem.' But his verbal acrobatics have had a long-lasting legacy. Article 4 of the Irish Constitution still declares, simply: 'The name of the State is Éire, or in the English language, Ireland.'

Even after the Constitution was adopted, for some years the Irish State continued its membership of the British Commonwealth. It was only in 1948 that the Republic of Ireland Act was passed, section 2 of which states: 'It is hereby declared that the description of the State shall be the Republic of Ireland'. Ironically, it was not Fianna Fáil – the republican party – which introduced this Act, but a government led by Taoiseach John A. Costello of Fine Gael.

The new Taoiseach announced his intention to declare the State a republic at a press conference in Canada on 7 September 1948, after winning an election that after 16 years finally saw Fianna Fáil out of office. The Republic of Ireland Act was formally inaugurated on 18 April (Easter Monday) 1949, and was presented as an almost technical legislative measure. As the Taoiseach said during the second stage of the Bill: '[It]...will put beyond all doubt, dispute and controversy our international status and our constitutional position. It will also, we hope and sincerely believe, end all that crescendo of bitterness which has been poisoning our country for the past 25 or 26 years, and it will also enable us to do that which, from the discussions which have already taken place in Dáil Éireann on the Bill, is the earnest hope of all Parties in this Parliament, improve our relations not merely with Canada, Australia, New Zealand and South Africa, but particularly with our nearest neighbour and best customer, Great Britain.'[61]

In other words, the basis for the status of the Irish Republic is statutory and not constitutional. Notably, this 'description' of the State as a republic does not change the name of the State, which as we know from Article 4 of the Constitution is simply 'Ireland.' Thus, since 1937 and even since 1948, the official name for the State is just that – 'Ireland'. This difference between the name of the State and its description has led to various legal difficulties. In 1989, for example, in the Ellis case, Judge Walsh condemned the UK courts for referring in extradition warrants to 'the Republic of Ireland.'[62] He said that if foreign courts issue warrants in English, they must refer to the State according to its name in English – that is, 'Ireland' – in accordance with Article 4. Further, he ruled that warrants that did not comply with this requirement should be returned to Britain for rectification by the courts there.

This persisting distinction between the name and description of our State is confusing and unwieldy, which may be one reason why the expert Constitution Review Group recommended in 1996 that, to simplify matters, the English language text of Article 4 should be amended to read 'The name of the State is Ireland' with the Irish language text to declare '*Éire is ainm don Stát.*'[63] This obvious step has not yet been taken, and in any case would still not confer constitutional status upon the description of Ireland as a republic. Thus, the legal status of Ireland as a republic is unrecognised constitutionally.

The question, however, may be asked whether this anomaly matters in practice, since Ireland is de facto a republic, whatever the legal name or description of the State as it appears in the Constitution. The answer is that the failure of the Constitution to identify the legal status of the State might be forgiven as a merely formal omission, but unfortunately it reflects a more basic truth: that our status as a republic is contestable, for a number of reasons, among them that the Constitution has failed adequately to ensure implementation of the separation of powers doctrine. It is proposed to address this issue in more detail.

Another obvious reason for contesting republican status is that, as argued further below, the Constitution does not provide for the true separation of Church and State essential for a functioning republic.

The Separation of Powers

It is argued that there has been a real breakdown of the separation of powers in our system. One aspect of the principle is enshrined in Article 15 of our Constitution, which states that: 'The sole and exclusive power of making laws for the State is hereby vested in the Oireachtas.' But the problem is that Irish legislators have been most inactive in many areas, thereby thrusting a lawmaking role upon judges. The courts have had to step into the breach in the context of governmental and legislative failures to enact law on abortion; to provide an adequate immigration policy; to protect the rights of asylum seekers or Irish-born children; or to meet the requirements of children with special needs or children at risk. Only late in 2012 was the Constitution finally amended to provide specific protection for the rights of children in the newly inserted Article 42A.

It could even be argued that in some cases judges have asserted popular sovereignty where both legislature and executive have notably failed. The decision in the *Crotty* case, for example, established the need to hold a referendum on entry into international obligations impacting on national sovereignty.[64] But this is arguably not an appropriate role for judges to play, except as a last resort. Judges in a country with a written Constitution clearly must have a strong protective role against legislative abuse of power, and against breaches of citizens' rights – but to require them to step in just because of legislative inertia is another matter.

Judicial lawmaking of this kind can lead to uneasy and unsatisfactory compromises on policy matters, with a strong element of uncertainty likely to arise, and a real tension likely to develop between the legislative and judicial functions. This sort of compromise does not ultimately make for good or effective policies in difficult areas, where democratic debate, conducted through the legislature, is really needed in order to achieve a more adequate resolution. Nor does it make for a properly functioning republic in the classic meaning of the term. The source of this problem may not, however, lie in the text of the Constitution, but rather in how its interpretation and application has developed over many decades.

The Question of Religion

The second significant change necessary to bring the Constitution forward is the removal of the religious references from the text. The distinctly theocratic aspect of the Irish State in previous times is reflected in the text, and within the historical development of our legal system. Prior to the Anglo-Norman invasion of 1170, a sophisticated indigenous system of law known as Brehon law prevailed. This was associated with a system of tribal kings or provincial chiefs, and an important place was reserved for the early Christian Church. Triad 200 sums up Brehon governance as comprising 'the three rocks to which lawful behaviour is tied: monastery, lord, kin.'[65]

The powerful place of the early Christian Church in Brehon law is mirrored by the powerful place of the Catholic Church in the emergence of the modern Irish republic. The Church has wielded considerable power for a long time in Ireland. Particularly in the late eighteenth century, the drastic restrictions imposed upon the rights of Catholics merely strengthened the Church's position in society, and the will of the people to practise their chosen faith. Catholicism thus became the religion of social and political defiance, of nationhood and patriotic identity – a heady cocktail indeed.

Once Catholic emancipation was formally secured, the Church amassed significant power, gaining ownership and control of many schools, hospitals and social services across Ireland. After independence, it moved into alignment with those in power in the new Free State, making its influence felt in every sphere of public life. As Maura Adshead has written, 'The Irish State, from the beginning, was ostentatiously Catholic.'[66]

Even now, the Catholic Church continues to act as a sort of 'shadow welfare state', supplanting the State's role in many ways. It also continues to hold vast tracts of valuable land and to wield great social and political power, despite the scandals over the sexual and physical abuse of children in the care and control of Catholic religious orders, and despite grave public concern over the way in which the Church attempted for so long to protect abusers within its ranks.

It is no coincidence that the President and members of the judiciary are required to take an oath beginning 'In the presence of Almighty God ...' and that the national broadcaster still carries a denominational religious message, the Angelus, at 6 p.m. every evening. No wonder that when we speak of 'Church and State', 'Church' always comes first.

This deference to religion elsewhere in Irish society is reflected in the bias of the constitutional text, the Preamble of which begins 'in the name of the Most Holy Trinity ...'. Article 6 provides that 'All powers of government, legislative, executive and judicial, derive, under God, from the people ...'. Again, these references may be dismissed as mere rhetorical flourishes that lack any real effect. However, to take this view is to overlook the symbolic importance of the text itself – one only need think of the recent controversy over whether reference to 'God' should be included in the preamble to the proposed European Constitution, to realise that these things do matter.

The religious influence on the wording of the fundamental rights Articles 40 to 44 is also especially notable. Article 41 represents perhaps the best example of this, providing special protection for the 'Family' (interpreted to mean only the family based upon marriage), and in Article 41.2 provides that 'by her life within the home, woman gives to the State a support without which the common good cannot be achieved.' The same Article commits the State to 'endeavour to ensure that mothers shall not be obliged by economic necessity to engage in labour to the neglect of their duties in the home.'

In a number of cases, beginning in 1963 with *Ryan v Attorney General*,[67] the courts invoked a 'natural law' doctrine of interpretation to imply rights into the Constitution. This had the positive effect of breathing life into the previously underused fundamental rights Articles, but at times it appeared as if judges were simply drawing rights out of the air, from their own subjective moral or religious beliefs. The source of natural rights for some judges was expressly theological, derived from Christian, or more particularly Catholic, teaching.

Thus, a theocratic ideology influenced in some respects the emerging constitutional rights jurisprudence. It also allowed the personal prejudices of individual judges to be reflected in their legal decisions. In perhaps the most notorious example, Chief Justice O'Higgins in the 1984 *Norris* case described homosexuality as 'unnatural sexual conduct which Christian teaching held to be gravely sinful.'[68]

The practice of invoking natural rights was finally expressed as falling out of judicial favour in 1995. That year, the Supreme Court upheld the constitutionality of legislation regulating the provision of information on abortion, saying that natural law cannot take priority over the text of the Constitution.[69]

But while natural law is certainly less frequently invoked now, judges may still have reference to 'higher law' principles in order to assist with constitutional interpretation. For example, in 1995, the Supreme Court held that a gastrostomy tube could be removed from a woman patient who had been in a near-persistent vegetative state for twenty-two years. In coming to this decision, the Court referred to religious principles, noting the concept of the 'intrinsic sanctity of life' in deciding that 'a view that life must be preserved at all costs does not sanctify life.'[70] Notably, however, the High Court did not extend this principle to encompass a right to assisted suicide, ruling against an applicant who sought to assert this right in January 2013.[71]

Thus, although natural law theories no longer have the influence over judicial interpretation of the Constitution that they once had, it would be inaccurate to suggest that contemporary constitutional interpretation comprises an exclusively secular approach. Rather, it appears that religious thinking or natural law doctrine may continue to have some bearing on future decisions.

The effect of the development of natural law doctrines by the judiciary has been to give judges a great deal more power than the framers of the Constitution might have intended – undermining the separation of powers doctrine, with judges essentially taking on a lawmaking role.

The Fundamental Rights Articles

Finally, it is argued that a radical revision of Articles 40–44 is necessary because of the restrictive nature of the ideology underlying those Articles. Apart from religious influences, liberal-democratic values are also strongly influential in the text of the fundamental rights provisions. The rights Articles emphasise the autonomy of the individual and ensure the protection of classic civil and political freedoms like the freedom of expression and the freedom of conscience or religion. Gerard Quinn has written in this context that 'Our Constitution pays homage to the ideology of theocracy as well as to the ideology of liberal-democracy.' He asserts that while the ideological tensions between these competing belief systems were only implicit in the past, they are coming increasingly to light as 'the economic conditions come into existence that make liberal-democracy a credible ideology in this country ... as a market society comes to maturity.'[72] In his view, theocratic principles have become marginalised in more recent constitutional jurisprudence, due to increased economic prosperity and greater acceptance of a market-generated philosophy of individualism, namely capitalism.

This author has argued similarly elsewhere that 'the fundamental rights Articles of the Constitution have their genesis in an uneasy blend of Catholic social teaching and a late nineteenth-century liberal philosophy. The conflict between these ideologies has never been fully resolved.'[73] The problem is that neither ideology gives sufficient weight to the sort of rights that might make a real difference to the lives of those who are most disadvantaged – those in any society in greatest need of protection of their rights. Where in the Constitution is recognition of the right to shelter, to healthcare, to social security provision?

The established body of socio-economic rights that has developed and is now protected in international rights instruments is simply not acknowledged in the enforceable provisions of the 1937 text, but rather is relegated to Article 45, tagged on as a concession to a socialist or social democratic view of society. Entitled 'Directive Principles of Social Policy,' the provisions of Article 45 are supposed to act as guidance to the legislature, but do not allow citizens to enforce them through the courts. The Article expresses a commitment to ensuring that 'the ownership and control of the material resources of the community may be so distributed amongst private individuals and the various classes as best to subserve the common good,' but this noble phrase has been largely ignored, both by the legislature and indeed by the courts. No definition has ever been developed as to the meaning of the 'common good', nor has any court sought directly to hold the State to its pledge to 'safeguard with especial care the economic interests of the weaker sections of the community', nor to 'protect the public against unjust exploitation.'

Future Directions for the Constitution

The arguments set out above make the case for a radical revision of the Constitution. The question is how a newly written Constitution could look. The fundamental rights Articles could be rewritten in order to make equality the core norm (as in the South African Constitution); to provide for a broader definition of 'family' than the narrow model adopted in Article 41; and to delete Article 40.3.3 in its entirety. In addition, a less elevated notion of private property protection could be advanced, with greater emphasis upon protection for freedom of association and for socio-economic rights like the right to housing or shelter, and the right to healthcare and social assistance.

Critics may argue that to implement this fundamental rewriting process would be to enshrine a very particular left-wing ideology within the document. In truth, however, a Constitution cannot be a value- or politics-neutral document. By definition, conceptions of rights are both political and politicised. It has been attempted here to show that the Constitution is not currently a neutral document – it already enshrines a very particular set of ideological beliefs that are no longer appropriate in today's Ireland. Ireland is now a multicultural society, with an increasingly secular and diverse population. The fundamental law of the land should reflect this changing, more progressive society. Hopefully, even if it is not to be rewritten, future amendments to the Constitution should recognise the changing reality.

In years to come, our Constitution should embrace and enshrine the conception of Ireland as a community united behind the need to ensure basic individual freedoms for all, regardless of religion, class, gender, sexuality, race or nationality. Its invocation of the 'common good' should be premised on the 'core norm' of equality, rather than being based upon an outdated religious ethos, uneasily coupled with classic liberal-democratic principles. We might look to the model of the new South African Constitution, a dynamic text with a fundamental commitment to ensuring equality and the protection of socio-economic rights. And we might look back to the core principles of republicanism, in order to reclaim and reinvigorate the status of a 'republic' – in law and in reality.

The Constitutional Convention

That is the ideal vision of a truly and radically revised Constitution. However, the proposals currently in place for revision are more limited in nature. In April 2010, Labour Party leader Eamon Gilmore proposed at the party's annual conference in Galway that a Constitutional Convention should be established in order to prepare a revised Constitution in time for the centenary of the 1916 uprising. This Convention proposal was subsequently included in the Programme for Government drawn up between Fine Gael and Labour following the February 2011 General Election and the formation of a coalition government comprising both parties. In July 2012, motions were passed in both Dáil and Seanad to enable the establishment of this Convention, and it held its first meeting in December 2012.

The Convention consists of one hundred persons including a chairperson, Tom Arnold of Concern. There are sixty-six citizen members, who have been selected from the electoral register so as to reflect a representative sample of Irish society; there is a member of the NI Assembly from each of the political parties that have accepted the invitation (four members in total); and the remaining group are twenty-nine members of the Oireachtas, chosen to be representative of both Houses. This author is very proud to have been elected by the parliamentary Labour Party as a member of the Labour delegation, and indeed to have been asked to lead that delegation on the Convention.

The remit of the Convention is to consider, and make recommendations to the Houses of the Oireachtas on, a range of specific matters, within a designated time frame.

Within two months of the date of the first public hearing, the Convention must report and make recommendations on two preliminary matters, namely, the reduction of the presidential term of office to five years, and the reduction of the voting age from 18 to 17. Within ten further months, the Convention must provide a report and recommendations on six other specified matters:

(a) review of the Dáil electoral system;
(b) giving citizens resident outside the State the right to vote in presidential elections;
(c) provision for same-sex marriage;
(d) amending the clause on the role of women in the home and encouraging greater participation of women in public life;
(e) increasing the participation of women in politics; and
(f) removal of the offence of blasphemy from the Constitution.

Finally, and again within one year of the date of the first public hearing (i.e., by December 2013), the Convention may report on such other relevant constitutional amendments as may be recommended by it. The Government is committed to providing in the Oireachtas a response to each recommendation of the Convention within four months and, if it accepts the recommendation, must indicate the time frame envisaged for the holding of any related referendum.

Many commentators have expressed disappointment at what they argue is the highly limited scope of the

Convention – and many have expressed cynicism at the likelihood of any radical change as a result of the Convention. Those doubts are addressed here, and it is argued that despite the narrowly defined focus of the Convention, it holds real potential for reconstruction – and in particular for the reform or revision of certain key Articles in the 1937 Constitution that have been criticised earlier.

This convention represents the first attempt by any government to provide for a citizen-led programme of constitutional reform. There have been large numbers of other reports – notably the comprehensive 1996 expert-led Constitution Review Group report and the many reports of the Joint Oireachtas Committee on the Constitution – amounting to politician-led reviews. Again, many important and thoughtful proposals for reform were generated by those reports, and it may be anticipated that the new convention will draw heavily on the work done previously in other fora.

However, this convention is notably different. And its strength lies in its difference. First, in the fact that the majority of the one hundred members are laypersons, citizens selected randomly, subject only to the need for a representative sample. Second, it is different in the fact that its deliberations are very clearly time limited. The clock has already begun to tick. The first public hearing was held on 1 December 2012, which means that the Convention must have reported and made recommendations to the Oireachtas by 1 February 2013 on the two preliminary issues for consideration – namely, the reduction of the presidential term of office and of the voting age. Indeed, the work of the Convention on all the other issues must be completed by 1 December 2013.

Two Preliminary Issues

The two preliminary issues described above have been referred to scathingly by commentators as soft or easy issues, not worthy of serious examination – but this critique misses the point. These are not of course the most contentious or controversial issues, but they do merit serious examination.

The issue of the reduction of the voting age in particular has generated a great deal of debate and literature already. Article 16.1.2 of the Constitution sets the voting age at 18, but this has already been amended – in January 1973, when the voting age was lowered from 21. Interestingly, Article 16.1.1 still provides that 21 is the minimum age for a person to be eligible for membership of Dáil Eireann (and Article 12.4 provides that 35 is the minimum age of eligibility for the office of President).

In 2005, the TASC-led Democracy Commission, of which this author was a member, produced a report entitled 'Engaging Citizens: the case for democratic renewal in Ireland'. During the preparation of that report, the Commission carried out public meetings around the country, and one of the issues that provoked great passion and debate was that of reduction of the voting age. The report found that although low proportions of young adults indicated an intention to vote in surveys, and although almost 67% of young people aged 18–25 did not vote in the 1999 local and European Elections, it was wrong to assume that low turnout was due to apathy or lack of interest. Instead, many of those aged 20–24 who did not vote had faced procedural obstacles, through being registered away from their place of residence (this was a particular issue for students), or because they had not received their polling cards in time. The day of polling also appeared to have been a major block to youth participation. It should be noted, however, that the holding of the children's rights referendum on a Saturday in November 2012 did not increase voter turnout.

The National Youth Council has also taken a position on the reduction of the voting age. In February 2012, the Council held a conference in Dublin entitled 'Vote@16 – Young People Young Voters – Supporting Active Citizenship', as part of an EU 'structured dialogue' process bringing together decision makers and young people throughout Europe to explore reducing the voting age for young people to 16 years. The 'Vote@16' campaign was also launched at the event. So there is already a degree of activism on the question of voter age – as reflected in the number of submissions already made to the Convention on this issue.

The other preliminary issue, that of reduction of the term of office of the presidency, is also worthy of serious consideration. Article 12.3.1 of the Constitution provides that 'The President shall hold office for seven years from the date upon which he enters upon his office…'. This term is lengthy by European standards, as most other EU member states with elected presidents have five-year terms as the norm. Most also have term limits, as we do, since under Article 12.3.2 a president is only eligible for re-election once. While there is unlikely to be any appetite for changing that provision, it is likely that a consensus may emerge from among the Convention members that seven years is too long.

Other Issues for the Convention – Reconstructive Potential

Once the Convention has reported on those two preliminary issues, as stated above it then has a further ten months to consider and report on six other specified issues, most of which are of serious import and some of which have already generated great controversy and debate – particularly the issue of marriage equality or same-sex marriage.

The review of the Dáil electoral system could of course generate a fundamental change to the very basic structures of our democracy, with the potential to consider radical changes like the introduction of a national list system to supplement or even replace the current set of geographical constituencies. It is unfortunate that the role of the Seanad has been relegated to an independent referendum, as it would have made more sense to consider both issues together. However, there is real potential for significant change under the heading of Dáil review.

Apart from the review of the Dáil system and the question of emigrants' votes, of the six specific issues under scrutiny, the other four relate to the fundamental rights Articles of the Constitution, the provisions that have been subjected to most criticism for reflecting a theocratic ideology. Article 41 has been singled out for much criticism, with its emphasis upon the 'Family' as possessing 'inalienable and imprescriptible rights,' and as the 'necessary basis of social order.' Article 41.3 pledges the State to 'guard with special care the institution of Marriage, on which the Family is founded.' However, 'marriage' is not defined in the text. In *Zappone & Gilligan v Revenue Commissioners*,[74] the High Court found that the word does not encompass same-sex couples, but the Supreme Court has never pronounced on this question definitively.

In any case, following its consideration of this issue, the Convention could now recommend a referendum to insert an inclusive definition of marriage to cover both gay and straight couples. This radical change would fundamentally undermine the conservative understanding of Article 41, and by implication the provisions of the rights protections generally. The elevated status given to the 'Family' would carry a very different meaning if 'Family' were to include those families based upon married same-sex partnerships.

Similarly, the Convention must also consider a significant further change to Article 41, which could again undermine the current conservatism inherent in its language. Indeed, it might be anticipated that the Convention will recommend changes to Article 41.2 of the Constitution to delete the outdated references to women's maternal role and to their 'life within the home'. The Constitution Review Group recommended in 1996 that these clauses should be replaced with a gender-neutral provision recognising the work of 'carers' in the home. If this change were to be made, together with the changes already made through the passing of the children's rights referendum, it would challenge the particularly religious ethos currently evident in the language of Articles 40–44.

Deleting the offence of blasphemy from Article 40.6.1 would also mean a significant improvement in the language of that provision – and would remove any rationale for the continuance in force of the much-criticised statutory offence of blasphemy introduced by former Justice Minister Dermot Ahern in section 36 of the Defamation Act 2009. Deletion of the offence should also highlight the need to remove other overt references to religion from the text of the Constitution – notably the religious oath required to be taken by those elected President, outlined in Article 12.8, which commences with the words 'In the presence of Almighty God…' and which ends 'May God direct and sustain me.'

In addition to the six specified issues, a ninth clause requires that the Convention may, following completion of the reports on those items, consider and report on any other relevant constitutional amendments that it may recommend. This general clause gives immense potential to an activist Convention, and campaigns are already being initiated by NGOs and voluntary groups to have particular matters included under this heading. Amnesty International, for example, has argued that the inclusion of specific protection for economic and social rights should be considered by the Convention. This change would be worthy of consideration, as inclusion of socio-economic rights would reflect contemporary conceptions of rights and give greater emphasis to the principles currently enshrined in Article 45. If this were done, it might enhance the power of the Constitution to deliver rights protection to those in need.

Even without that ninth clause, it is argued that real reconstruction of some of the most problematic provisions among the fundamental rights Articles may be carried out by this Convention. After all, most of the arguments that have been made for a radical overhaul of the Constitution have focused particularly upon the need to reform and revise the fundamental rights Articles. There is potential to do just that within the terms of this Convention – and its strength lies in the commitment to respond to each recommendation within a specified time frame.

Conclusion

Back in 2010, when the idea of a Constitutional Convention was first put forward, the prospect of a comprehensive review of the Constitution excited many people, particularly those on the left, and to many constitutional lawyers. It is an enticing prospect to consider rewriting provisions that hark back to a different Ireland – an Ireland dominated by the Catholic Church. Now in the twenty-first century, more than 75 years after its original enactment, it is widely acknowledged that we need a Constitution that reflects the new multi-cultural Ireland, that reflects the diversity and pluralism of our population and that no longer bows the head in genuflection to the ideologies of a particular religion.

The Convention that has now been established, with its narrower remit and specific focus, at first sight appears less exciting in the potential it can offer for reconstruction. However, on closer examination, the reforms that it must consider offer within them the prospect of bringing about real and radical change within the fundamental rights provisions in particular. This convention is what we make of it – both the members of the Convention, those who will be involved in speaking about it or working with it, and members of the public generally. It has the potential to bring about a dynamic set of changes to the 1937 text that may generate some real reconstruction along the lines of a truly republican document.

BEYOND LEGAL CONSTITUTIONALISM

Eoin Daly

Recent public debate on the Irish Constitution has focused primarily on what might be termed the necessary content of a republican Constitution. This is a theme on which the President in particular has encouraged reflection in the wake of the economic crisis and the apparent failure and dysfunctionality of many of our institutions. This discussion is obviously vital: in particular, there is a need for debate on the principles of equality and human rights, on the institutional and political systems and the overarching social values that are to be enshrined in the State's basic law. This is intimately related to a discussion around what it means to conceive of Ireland as a republican State and society – and indeed, how these values have evolved since the enactment of the present Constitution in 1937.

However, in this chapter I will focus not on the content of the republican Constitution, but rather its form. Republicanism as a political ideal – the idea of a self-governing community of equals – speaks, I believe, to the form of a Constitution as well as its content; indeed, they are inseparable to some extent.

Republicanism and Constitutional Form

In a sense, the form of the Irish Constitution is less obvious than its content. It is clear, for example, that the Constitution provides for a parliamentary democracy with cabinet government, a separation of powers, and various rights that are defined and limited in various ways. But what of its form? In Ireland, we have primarily a legal Constitution, and our conception of constitutionalism – both at expert and 'lay' levels – is predominantly legalistic.

This legal conceptualisation of the Constitution is significant from the republican perspective. Generally speaking, a 'Constitution' refers to the set of principles or norms governing the exercise of public power, the fundamental principles according to which a State is supposed to operate. We have a 'legal Constitution' because these principles and norms are codified in a legal form; they are given the force of law and are, generally speaking, enforceable by courts.[75] Law is, in Ireland, the main source of constitutional authority. Thus, it is generally taken for granted both that the Constitution is law, and that constitutional law is exhaustive of the Constitution. Moreover, students are taught that the 'Constitution' is a legal document they must learn to use and interpret as lawyers – that is, using technical, expert skills unavailable to others.

Yet 'legal constitutionalism' is far from self-evident. Constitutional principles might be rooted not in law, but in political traditions and conventions, internalised not only by officials but also to some extent by 'lay' citizens, and sanctioned not by courts but by the force of public morality. A Constitution need not, then, be legally codified

– this was very much the case with the Constitution of the ancient Roman republic,[76] and to some extent it is true also of the constitutional system of our closest neighbour, even today. Many of the key precepts of the British Constitution – parliamentary sovereignty, royal assent to legislation and the collective responsibility of the government – are grounded in and enforced by political convention, not by law – that is, by the expectations and norms of the broader political community – whereas the equivalent principles in the Irish Constitution are unambiguously 'legal',[77] and we look to courts to sanction and uphold them.

Historically, republicans – given their understanding of political freedom as self-government – have tended to be somewhat apprehensive of legal constitutionalism. The Constitution, from this perspective, must be in the ownership of the people, and its content a function of public deliberation, rather than being vested in the care of expert legal institutions. Rousseau perhaps went the furthest in insisting that the Constitution was sanctioned neither by courts nor even by official conventions, but ultimately through its internalisation in the dispositions of the people themselves. In *The Social Contract* he said that 'the most important kind of law of all [is] graven not in marble or in bronze, but in the heart of the citizens ... the State's genuine Constitution.'[78] Indeed, he thought that citizen virtues, based on public reason and the primacy of the common good, were the basis of the Constitution itself. Moreover, he thought that the primary function of the Constitution was to foster the virtues and dispositions in which republican politics could flourish – the Constitution was not a legal restraint on State power, but a project of social transformation, which would orient legislation towards the realisation of the common good.[79] Republican politics, he thought – the politics of the common good – could not flourish in a factional, alienated society, and so republican constitutionalism was, at root, a social project.

The main implication of legal constitutionalism is that constitutional principles acquire the force of law and so can be legally enforced by courts. The ultimate responsibility for deciding the meaning and content of the Constitution then lies with the courts. This is sometimes termed judicial supremacy – the subject of some debate in the United States.[80] In practical terms, the main consequence of this is the power of courts to strike down parliamentary legislation deemed to contravene their understanding of constitutional principles.[81] This conception is in fact novel, historically speaking. Even where European states enacted formal constitutions, this was not usually supported by any power of judicial review over legislation, based on a strong sense of parliamentary supremacy. With a few notable exceptions such as the United States, the now-dominant legal constitutionalism was not accepted in the West until after the Second World War – when the need for law to robustly contain political authority became particularly and acutely obvious. The creation of constitutional courts in nearly every continental European democracy, empowered to enforce entrenched constitutions against the vagaries of parliamentary politics, reflected this transformation in constitutional thought. But one of the main consequences of this development – and the reason it was resisted for so long – is the accretion to unelected judges of what essentially amounts to a form of political power. Constitutions are quite different from other legal instruments – they contain rather vague and open-ended principles of political right, whose content is contestable and clearly political: the power to interpret and apply these is clearly a form of political power. Despite constitutional interpretation often being presented as a morally and politically neutral exercise in objective legal logic, constitutional principles are sufficiently malleable and indeterminate to be read through a favoured ideological world view. Thus, historically, opposition to judicial power was usually strongest in progressive political movements, suspicious that constitutional principles might be used as insidious political weapons by an activist conservative judiciary – for example, the judges who reacted against Roosevelt's 'New Deal' in defence of property rights and the minimal state.

This political empowerment of courts might be considered the necessary price of ensuring a robust system of 'checks and balances' – of containing governmental power for the sake of individual freedom. Nevertheless, it creates a dilemma for republicanism as a political theory of self-government through representative institutions. From the republican perspective, legal constitutionalism might even, in fact, have certain virtues. On the one hand, instances of judicial activism might enhance the quality of public deliberation by provoking discussion on matters of public importance; thus, the 'conversation' between the legal and political branches of the State might enhance 'deliberative democracy'. More pertinently, judicial activism might also help to contain arbitrary power – it might be an important part of an overall system of robust 'checks and balances', in which the dispersal of power, between different institutions, helps to counteract and limit each, thus enhancing individual freedom. In particular, so-called constitutional review or judicial review might help to keep a check on the potentially dominating power of the Executive, especially in constitutional systems where executives tend to dominate the legislative agenda. In the context of a fused executive-legislature system, where the government tends to keep the lower House of Parliament under its thumb through the party whip system, legal constitutionalism might help to ensure a 'mixed Constitution' – a historic republican theme – this being born of a concern to ensure that no single organ wields uncontested, unchecked power. As Philip Pettit has put it, 'the people should rule themselves via the interaction of distinct assemblies and authorities, not via any single representative, individual or corporate.'[82] It is difficult to object to judicial activism in light of various examples of the courts robustly enforcing constitutional rights against political abuses – for example, in the Supreme Court's famous assertion of a (limited) constitutional right to use contraception.[83] Indeed, liberal, idealistic law students tend to hero-worship great judges as the protectors of freedom, and are correspondingly acculturated to be suspicious of 'politics' as a threat to freedom.

Yet insofar as judicial activism is valued as instrumental to individual freedom, this speaks to a very narrow and arguably redundant conception of 'freedom' itself. It has been often argued that republicanism embraces a distinctive and more morally plausible idea of freedom, compared to liberalism. For 'neo-republicans' such as

Philip Pettit and Quentin Skinner – drawing from the ideas of Ancient Roman republicanism – freedom is conceived of as non-domination, rather than as non-interference.[84] Primarily, it means that freedom is negated not simply by external interference in our choices or actions, but rather by our vulnerability to the arbitrary will of others – by having to live our lives according to the agenda of another. The mere capacity of others to interfere, arbitrarily, through unbounded and uncontested power, is inimical to republican freedom – even if that capacity is never exercised or inflicted. Power disparities within private relationships allow for the invigilation, or, as Pettit puts it, the 'alien control' of individuals' choices – even where this dominating power is clothed with formal consent or acquiescence. These uneven power relations force us to engage in strategies of fawning or self-censorship that entail 'unfreedom', even where we never directly suffer 'interference' as such.[85] Correspondingly, this conception of freedom as non-domination implies a more activist, even emancipatory role for the State. Moreover, the role of the courts in checking arbitrary State power, as well as protecting individuals from private oppression, might certainly enhance the enjoyment of freedom as non-domination in society.

On the other hand, however, the ideal of freedom as non-domination arguably does not capture the full breadth of republican political thought.[86] Republican aims cannot be understood purely in terms of freedom as a negative right – that is, in terms of the goal of limiting and containing the reach of State power over private individuals. Arguably, freedom as non-domination is in fact quite a conservative interpretation of the republican tradition. Republicanism can, alternatively, be understood as an ideal of self-government – a tradition illuminated by such diverse figures in the history of thought as James Harrington, Jean-Jacques Rousseau, Wolfe Tone, the English commonwealthmen of the seventeenth century, and, of course, the American and French revolutionaries of the eighteenth century.[87] In this tradition, freedom is realised through political participation – specifically, through equal membership within a self-governing community, free of internal as well as external domination. Self-government is realised through public deliberation on the common good, and the republican Constitution facilitates freedom as self-government by providing political devices through which equality of participation is encouraged and realised. Freedom is essentially political, and can only be realised in the context of a political community whose members are meaningful participants in that community.

Therefore, republicanism envisages that the body of citizens – a community of equals – participates in and scrutinises the processes of government, thus claiming ownership over the identity of our State and public life. For one branch of republican theory – the neo-republicanism discussed above – the values of political participation, contestation and civic virtue are not intrinsic or essential human goods: they are simply instrumental to freedom as non-domination, as the ultimate political goal. The conjecture is that wide participation and public deliberation are at least likely, in the long run, to secure a social and political order in which freedom as non-domination is consistently protected, through the contestation and scrutiny of State power. Yet political participation is not directly or intrinsically necessary to the enjoyment of freedom. However, for another school – loosely termed civic republicanism[88] and sometimes traced to Aristotle's civic humanism – freedom is inherently 'political' in a much deeper sense: participation in politics and government is intrinsic, rather than simply instrumental, to individual freedom. We are free to the extent that we are participants in our political community and in self-government. This might be conceptualised in terms of politics as a privileged conception of the good life or, more modestly, in light of the role of participation in human self-understanding. In this view, self-government through participation is not simply a strategy for containing State power and thus enhancing private freedoms; it is an end in itself. Putting it more simply, participation is not instrumental to freedom, it is constitutive of it.

Whether it views political participation as instrumental or intrinsic to human freedom, the republican vision presupposes an active citizenry, constantly engaged in public affairs. It envisages a society based around deliberation on the common good, and the active engagement of public reason in the sense of a widespread acceptance of the need for the public interest (admittedly a problematic concept) to be prioritised over private interests. Thus, society, as a scheme of social and political co-operation, is not simply conceived as a federation of atomised, disaggregated individuals based on the crude bargaining of private interests and utilities; nor is it depicted as an organic collective bound to a higher common purpose. Furthermore, popular participation is not valuable, in this lens, because it is thought likely to produce better decisions – although it might arguably ensure the interests of the governed are properly accounted for. Rather, it is valuable in itself – with the ideal of freedom then being realised through equal membership in the self-governing community.

Thus, for republicans, freedom is not secured in the vacuum of power; rather, it is realised through the status of citizenship itself.[89] As outlined, there are important analytical differences within republican thought. For neo-republicanism, freedom is defined negatively: it consists of the absence of domination, and civic participation is valuable only because it is instrumental in protecting citizens, ultimately, from arbitrary power. But civic republicanism embraces a thicker ideal – that of civic participation as a valuable good in itself. We are free insofar as the laws that bind us and the institutions that govern us are truly our own, where the constraints upon us are the product of our own deliberation, as equals, on our common good – not simply in the sense that there are formal procedures in place through which the will of the majority is effectuated, but where – as equals – we enjoy the means and resources to participate in and influence the processes of government. For Rousseau, the dilemma of political theory was how we could submit ourselves to political authority and law, yet remain 'as free as before', in his famously elusive phrase.[90] His equally elusive solution lay in the concept of the 'general will' – the will of a political community founded on social contract, transcending any calculus of private interests amongst its individual members. The general will is accessible to citizens who are capable of exercising a form of public reason – of engaging in public affairs on common terms, independently of their contingent features and resources. Thus, republicanism presupposes the possibility of ordinary persons internalising deliberative constraints on their political demands – a society based around justice rather than utility.

Of course, the realisation of self-government under the 'general will', or even the common good, has an air of political fantasy at worst, or at least of unrealism. It presupposes the exercise of almost unimaginable levels of civic virtue – of the sort that could only exist, perhaps, in small, cohesive societies – or which, more darkly, would require intolerable forms of State coercion. More modestly, the aim of political freedom as equal participation in the self-governing community requires a degree of social equality for its effective realisation. The equality needed for genuine participation is not simply a formalistic conception of 'equality before the law' – which ignores the corrosive and exclusionary effects of the unequal distribution of power, wealth and opportunity. The republican vision of substantive equality requires that nobody is subject to domination by dint of disparities of social and economic power, and that an excessive concentration of wealth and economic power does not lead to the appropriation of public authority for the narrow purposes of a powerful minority. In Ireland in particular, the constitutional conception of equality that has prevailed has been the formalistic 'equality before the law' view – it has always been assumed that socio-economic equality, beyond the purview of republican constitutionalism, must be pursued and mediated through 'ordinary' politics.[91]

This republican conception of freedom is certainly very different from that of the nineteenth century liberals – which is arguably still influential today. For liberals such as Jeremy Bentham, freedom – conceived in a rather sterile and narrow way – was, echoing Hobbes, thought to mean no more than the absence of external obstruction upon the exercise of will.[92] Many simply believed that 'rights' claims, in politics, simply obscured what were, at root, competing claims of utility: 'natural' or 'fundamental' rights, transcending utility or preference, were famously derided as 'nonsense on stilts'. Indeed, British constitutional discourse is still marked by a certain degree of scepticism towards 'rights talk'.

For many of these liberals, what mattered was not ultimately the authorship, ownership or control of laws, but whether they enhanced our utility, defined subjectively to each of us. One could theoretically be as 'free' under a benign despot as under a participative republican regime – as long as the State would leave us to our private ends as far as possible.[93] For those liberals who thought freedom consisted of the 'silence of the laws', the public good was not a common good, but merely an aggregation of the utilities of disaggregated, atomistic individuals, who had no common purpose or project other than the pursuit of private utility itself.

Republicanism, however, focuses not solely on the effects on private welfare, of laws and State actions, but also their ownership and control – on participation in the definition and construction of our terms of social co-operation. It defines freedom not solely in terms of the absence of power, but also with reference to the intrinsic good of participation in public affairs. Thus, with its unrelenting focus on participation for the common good, republicanism offers a potent antidote to classical liberalism's sterile, alienating and redundant concept of freedom. Liberal freedom says 'leave me alone'; republican freedom says 'let us participate'.

Problematising Legal Constitutionalism

Why should legal constitutionalism concern republicans? In summary, the ideal of the self-governing community of equals – that is, the idea that the power imposed on us must in some sense be our own – means that the Constitution, being at once the State's basic law and its basic identity, must be a function of popular deliberation, scrutiny and consent.

This, in turn, must mean something other than the power of the people to vote on the text of the Constitution and its amendments. Of course, although we have a 'legal Constitution' in Ireland, its content was voted for by the people in the 1937 plebiscite and in the subsequent amending referenda. However, formal approval of constitutional content through a majority vote is not the same as genuine common deliberation on the State's basic law. Formal plebiscitary exercises are no substitute for genuine deliberation and engagement. While it might intuitively seem more inclusive to have legislation directly approved by voters, merely being invited to vote 'Yes' or 'No' might, from the republican viewpoint, require little engagement or deliberation from the citizen – a simulacrum of civic participation. The use of frequent referenda might in fact be quite consistent with a liberal, atomised – profoundly un-republican – society, with little public engagement or deliberation on questions of the common good, a society marred by complacency and civic withdrawal. The referendum ritual might, indeed, exemplify choice without deliberation – whereby we can simply communicate a preference without first being forced to deliberate and compromise, and those private preferences are then aggregated to an expression of majoritarian democracy. Whereas deliberation and related forms of civic participation are quintessentially republican, referenda actually seem more redolent of liberal 'choice', with all its potent, mystifying force.

Arguably, the current referendum mechanism operates very much as a formal rubberstamp for decisions whose content, effectively, is decided without public deliberation. The referendum is a binary choice, the right to say 'Yes' or 'No'. There is no power, as exists elsewhere, for citizens to initiate referenda through petition.[94] Despite this, it may nonetheless have a great deal of value in containing and checking the power of the political organs, which could amend the Constitution of the Irish Free State (1922–37) more or less at will. The referendum is no more than a veto – it is simply the final step in a broader procedure, which starts with the government sponsoring a bill in the lower house. This also means the referendum is hardly the dangerously 'populist' instrument it is so often derided as, because it is so procedurally couched and preceded by parliamentary approval.

Conversely, the citizens have virtually no input in formulating what amendments are actually proposed. Often, it seems their choice is reduced to that of resentful veto or resigned acquiescence. The original text, although unenthusiastically approved by plebiscite, was in fact drafted by a relatively closed coterie (although not simply by Dev and John Charles McQuaid as is often imagined). One might have thought that the Constitutional Convention would have signalled a break from this practice of constitutional amendments being handed down from on high for formal approval. However, its deliberately and cynically narrow remit makes this seem hollow, particularly in comparison to the impressive process of constitutional reform recently undertaken in Iceland.[95]

Despite the relatively modest empowerment that the constitutional referendum affords citizens, there is a great deal of emphasis, in constitutional discourse and case law, on the 'sovereignty of the people' as an ultimate constitutional principle. For example, in the Supreme Court judgment *Re Article 26 and the Regulation of Information (Services Outside the State for Termination of Pregnancies) Bill 1995*, Hamilton CJ asserted: 'the Constitution … is the fundamental and supreme law of the State representing … the will of the People.'[96]

Yet seen in light of the reality of our politics, this sense of 'popular sovereignty' seems something of an empty incantation. It conveys a sense of control or empowerment that does not exist in reality. This 'sovereignty' doctrine sees the 'people' genuflected to as the ultimate source of constitutional authority because of their unfettered right to amend (or preserve) the Constitution. But this is merely a sort of self-satisfied fiction – it implies that the content of the Constitution somehow emanates from the popular will, simply because its provisions can be traced, at some point, to an acquiescing ballot. That mythology of popular sovereignty is extremely misleading because it serves only to obscure the real dynamics of power underlying the content and operation of the Constitution. It misleadingly portrays political choice as somehow being in the ultimate command of the idealised 'people', based on what effectively amounts to little more than a veto power on constitutional change. On the other hand, while the referendum might not realistically embody the romanticised notion of 'popular sovereignty', it may nonetheless be valued not only as a check on political power, but also as an instrument for encouraging wide participation in and deliberation on public affairs – this being the ultimate normative horizon of republican politics. One of the key functions of republican constitutionalism is to provide mechanisms that foster participation by citizens in public affairs and deliberation on the common good. The referendum, for all its limitations, is one of a precious few constitutional devices that prompt citizens outside professional politics to deliberate and participate, beyond the framework of periodical elections.

So far, I have dealt with the widespread idea, in legal discourse, that the constitutional text embodies or captures the 'will of the people'. Yet while it is misleading to claim that the 'people' somehow control or determine the text of the Constitution, its text is not, in any event, synonymous with its meaning or content. While the text and the amendments are in reality formulated by governments, on legal advice, and subsequently lent the imprimatur of popular legitimacy through plebiscitary ratification, the ultimate meaning of the Constitution – as a concrete set of propositions – is ultimately thought to be a matter of legal expertise. This is partly because constitutional propositions – claims about what the Constitution means or requires – are yielded from overlapping provisions and are rarely self-evident or even foreseeable based on the texts citizens vote on.

In any event, this is the main reason legal constitutionalism is problematic from the republican perspective. It shrouds the content of the basic law in the mystique of legal expertism, and correspondingly works against the ideal that it should be somehow in the ownership of the citizen body – a function of public deliberation on the common good. It disarms and negates the political, entrusting constitutional deliberation to a relatively closed caste. As outlined earlier, constitutions, including the Irish Constitution, tend to consist not solely of technical rules concerning institutional competences, but also vague, open-textured statements that are susceptible to being read in the lens of – or marshalled in the service of – one's preferred ideology or world view. Thus, legal constitutionalist terminology tends to clothe ideology with the air of legal objectivity: often, it is simply politics insidiously masquerading as a separate, neutral mode of reasoning. The Constitution is a legal charter, but it contains interpretive, malleable ideals – such as the principle of equality before the law, and the proclamation that Ireland is a 'sovereign and democratic' State[97] – which are amenable to being used to rationalise a plurality of contradicting propositions and outcomes. These are not typical legal rules, but rather principles of political right that judges are empowered to interpret and apply – and ultimately clothe with 'legal' authority.

On the one hand, this is problematic because it means that a portion of political choice is divested from representative and politically accountable institutions and vested in ostensibly non-political – or at least non-accountable – personages, namely, the courts. This is why historically, 'republican' regimes – with few exceptions – were reluctant to cede courts any power to review the constitutionality of legislation (and correspondingly, why formal, codified constitutions provided no real fetter upon political organs). This is the focal point of much of the literature on 'political constitutionalism' hostile to judicial empowerment, for example, the work of British republican scholars such as Adam Tomkins and Richard Bellamy, as well as American scholars sceptical of judicial review in the United States context.[98] For Waldron, and other critics, judicial review degrades public deliberation whereby a 'star-struck people may speculate about what the Supreme Court will do next.'[99] To this, Eisgruber retorts that citizens are effectively little more than 'spectators' in the case of electoral democracy as well, but that at least 'in the case of constitutional adjudication they will be spectators to an argument about moral and political principle, rather than to an interest group deal.'[100]

However, on the other hand, arguably this divesting of power from representative institutions should not be regarded as the most important focus of republican opposition to legal constitutionalism. More pertinently, the legal form of the Constitution gives rise to a peculiar and corrosive perception of constitutional meaning. This perception, specifically, is that the principles of political right the Constitution contains – and how they interact with each other to yield concrete propositions of constitutional law – are treated as questions of legal knowledge. Legal knowledge, in this sense, is depicted as a separate and distinctive mode of reasoning, which is inaccessible and indecipherable to the 'laity'. In this view, interpreting the political principles of the Constitution is seen as a lawyerly skill not entirely dissimilar to the expert skill involved in interpreting a statute or a contract. Interpreting these legally codified principles of political right is depicted as a form of expert technical knowledge, a neutral search for objective truth, which lies only in the hands of those qualified. The consequence of this is, in some sense, to divest these matters from the political – putting them beyond the purview of political deliberation. This arguably diminishes the vitality and relevance of public discourse, political argument being negated by expert terminologies: contestable matters of public interest are captured by sages.

To illustrate this rather abstract point, constitutional argument has a way of disarming the lay interlocutor, which should worry republicans. For example, if a newspaper polemic argues that a particular policy, practice or law violates one or other of our fundamental political values, any 'lay' citizen can engage with, consider and oppose such an argument. Yet where it argues that the same state of affairs is unconstitutional, this lends an expertist gloss to what is often, at root, implicitly an ideological position, but one that legal constitutionalism allows to be presented as a neutral, quasi-scientific proposition. Examples might include the argument that withholding the subsidy for fee-charging schools, or gender quotas in politics, are unconstitutional.[101] In reality, legal authorities can be marshalled to rationalise contradictory propositions or arguments, and this is peculiarly true of constitutional law. Sometimes, a practice will be blatantly in contravention of a specific, literal constitutional rule. In reality, however, the Constitution is vague enough to provide legalistic rationalisations for a multitude of contradictory political and normative stances. Thus, legal constitutionalism veils a certain sort of politics – implicitly, the dominant politics of the judiciary and the legal professions – while simultaneously disarming and divesting the political. Legal argumentation in the constitutional realm is insidiously ideological, because we cannot interpret vague linguistic formulations of political right without in some sense bringing our values and priorities to bear in reading it. For example, the question of whether the constitutional principle of freedom of association should exempt private clubs from equality legislation depends on a more or less intuitive 'balancing' or weighing-up exercise, as between competing constitutional considerations, which masks substantive value judgements. Yet on the other hand, constitutional interpretation's essentially non-neutral nature is obscured through the deployment of expert legal terminology – for example, judges portraying statutory interpretation as an exercise in recovering the 'intention of the legislature', or, indeed, constitutional interpretation as the discovery of the mythical 'will of the people'. It is also obscured in the bogus legal terminology of 'balance' and 'proportionality' as supposedly apolitical, neutral concepts of law, which mask substantive normative judgments.

Another example is the argument that same-sex marriage is unconstitutional – which is to say, that it is removed from political and legislative choice. The assertion that marriage as envisaged in the Constitution is a necessarily heterosexual institution is in no sense the product of neutral legal expertise. Indeed, there is no reason to believe that the meaning of concepts like 'sovereignty', 'equality' or cven 'marriage' should be exclusively the concern of lawyers. Yet in Ireland – far more so than in the US or the UK – public figures and institutions seem to accept rather uncritically the damaging myth that lawyers' interpretation of constitutional principle is the product of a technical, ideologically neutral form of expertise. Arguably, this model of constitutionalism – the deployment of constitutional interpretation as a trump in political argument – stifles legitimate political choice and disempowers the political generally. On the other hand, this difficulty is attenuated somewhat in Ireland because our Constitution can be amended easily, and so at least the people can overrule, in theory, judges' interpretations of constitutional principle. For example, a referendum reversed a rather doctrinaire Supreme Court judgment that the Constitution implicitly accorded absolute Cabinet confidentiality.[102] However, political and practical considerations limit the degree to which referenda can be used to reverse unpopular judgments.

In any event, what is most problematic is the fact that, unlike legislation or government policy, judicial interpretations of constitutional principle do not have the quality of popular contestability: they are shrouded in the mystique of expertise. For example, in the case *McGee v Attorney General* [1972],[103] Justice Brian Walsh effectively claimed that under the Constitution, 'justice', or so-called 'natural law', is 'superior to positive law', and that it falls to judges – 'in light of their training and experience' – to determine what justice or natural law consists of. The outcome of the case – an implied constitutional right to use contraception in marriage – seemed liberal and progressive. However, the judgment, perhaps the high-water mark of 'judicial activism' in recent Irish history, could be read as an extraordinary judicial arrogation of political authority – a claim that judicial power is not only the power to apply legal authorities to adjudicate cases, but to appropriate the content of justice and political right itself. It deployed, moreover, the mystifying terminology of 'natural law' – the theological lodestar for what is deemed inevitable, universal and eternal within our contingent social order. It seems almost trite to point out that what, to a judge, seems natural or self-evident will often reflect their peculiar background and life experience. However, it must be acknowledged that in the four decades since this case, Supreme Court judges have retreated from this bold stance, and have repeatedly affirmed the necessity of judicial self-restraint within a democratic constitutional framework.[104]

Arguably, in any event, this idea of judges as the ultimate custodians and expositors of the Constitution represents ideology in the sense of a viewpoint falsely presenting itself as natural and self-evident, rather than as the product of a contingent, peculiar social structure. Under this almost juristocratic vision of constitutionalism, our polity's normative identity is in some sense spirited out of the realm of public deliberation, and appropriated – not so much by judges as such, but by the expertism of lawyers generally: lawyers who often disarm lay interlocutors with constitutional argumentation. Moreover, in legal discourse and legal education in Ireland, there is an extraordinary faith not only in legal constitutionalism as the bedrock of the 'rule of law', but also in the proposition that constitutional content is apolitically derived and discovered. 'Politics', grubby and venal, is seen as the main threat to freedom, and 'law' – somehow above or beyond politics, and embodying superior virtues – is thought to be its cure. In this vision, lawyers will save the people from the folly of their own populism – implicitly, from their unsuitability for self-government.

Therefore, the main 'republican' problem with legal constitutionalism is not so much that it disempowers the elected Parliament to pass whatever legislation it wishes. Rather, it is that legal constitutionalism, in the sense in which I have defined it, rests on the false and harmful belief that the content and meaning of constitutional principle – and therefore, of the political identity of our State – is, by necessity, vested in trained experts and, correspondingly, divested from the laity. This has necessary consequences for our conception of citizenship: indirectly at least, it degrades the idea of popular sovereignty understood as wide participation in and deliberation on public affairs. Insofar as our State is defined as 'republican', we must ourselves participate in the definition of what rights are and how they are ordered with each other – this cannot be handed down to us from on high.

Admittedly, this claim creates a tension with another democratic ideal – that is, the principle that competing political visions should be mediated within an overarching, entrenched legal framework that transcends the vagaries of ordinary politics. Of course it is essential to our liberties that at least certain constitutional rules surrounding the functioning of our institutions are legally codified – that they do not belong to 'ordinary politics'. This is a troubling paradox: politics must be set within a constitutional frame, but constitutionalism is itself inherently political. Perhaps we cannot have it both ways. Certainly, however, the prevailing conception of constitutionalism in Ireland is almost naively legalistic. It is particularly naive to believe that our political liberty over the long run can be entrusted to a robust judicial activism – to the benign efforts of an idealised liberal vanguard of enlightened jurists. Political freedom, I have argued, does not require simply the containment of State power in its reach over private choice and private autonomy, although these are important. In this image, 'law' – the realm of reason and rationality, contains 'politics', seen as the realm of baser, grubby passions. Rather, political freedom consists in public ownership of and participation in the processes of government, through which we elevate ourselves above the crude interplay of aggregate private interest, and govern ourselves according to the ideal of the common good. Ultimately, then, political liberty in the long run depends on there being an active, vigilant citizenry – and that may in ways be undermined by the particular vision of legal constitutionalism we have adopted in Ireland. This ideal of the active, vigilant citizenry, that claims control and ownership over the terms of our political association, is a formative project: it is itself the product of political and constitutional choice, and its realisation is the task of constitutional design. The object of republican constitutionalism must not be solely that of containing and limiting State power, but, rather, of encouraging wide participation in public affairs and popular engagement on questions of the common good. The referendum is arguably one such mechanism, but it is insufficient in and of itself.

Arguably, the prevailing conception of law and lawyers in Ireland is the closest thing we have to a secular clericalism. Lawyers are imagined either as sages emerging from conclave, divining unfathomable constitutional propositions presumed to be beyond the lay mind, or as clinical, scientific figures, engaged in the search for neutral 'solutions'. Despite what many lawyers will claim, propositions of constitutional right mask deeper ideological and political commitments. Yet constitutional expertise succeeds in self-mystification to an extraordinary degree in Ireland. A good starting point for a republican narrative on the social role of law might be an acknowledgment of a tendency to take constitutional lawyers and constitutional advice slightly too seriously – to take at face value motley affirmations of constitutional principle as if these were the exclusive knowledge of a technocratic, expert caste of legal scientists. That reduces citizens to spectators. Amongst a certain breed of lawyers, there is an implicit but clear cultural disdain for the whole enterprise of politics – with this cynicism translating, conversely, as an excessive faith in judicial power and legal wisdom. The self-conception of lawyers is sometimes that of a proud phalanx of defenders of liberty. If only law can contain the excesses of the political, then liberty will flourish – an unfortunate saviour complex that overlooks political participation as the ultimate horizon of freedom. This ignores the question of how political freedom, understood as participation in self-government, is undermined by the insidious status hierarchies that seem to more or less spontaneously emerge in liberal social orders. Perhaps we need to seriously consider the arguments put forward by Mark Tushnet in his provocatively entitled book, *Taking the Constitution Away from the Courts*.[105] This might be the starting point for a discussion on how constitutionalism can, in the republican lens, be divested from expertist appropriation.

Conclusion

As I have argued, republican constitutionalism ultimately contains a troubling paradox: while the legal entrenchment of principles of political right helps to keep a check on power, it correspondingly cedes a portion of political authority to expert appropriation, and correspondingly divests it from the people as a community of citizens. There seems to be an inevitable trade-off between two important republican principles – on the one hand, the containment of arbitrary dominating power through robust checks and balances transcending ordinary politics, and on the other, the ideal of self-government, by a community of equals, through deliberation on the common good. This is perhaps another expression of the tension between individual liberty and democratic self-government: the people must be able to determine the principles and policies on the basis of which their community is governed, but individual freedom requires that some choices be put beyond the reach of political change. Perhaps this is too pessimistic; in any event, I argue this is the main theoretical challenge for the republican constitutionalists of the twenty-first century.

Our Constitution and our Politics: Why Political Culture Matters and Constitutional Text Does Not!

Tom Hickey

Section I

The notion of 'constitutional reform' seems to evoke something foundational. In the case of a constitutional amendment, the general perception is that great change in the area in question will follow. The corollary is that a whole new text would bring about a new social and political order. And yet, in the greater scheme of things, there is very little in a typical 'liberal-democratic' constitution. It may refer to some fundamental values of a people. It will establish the institutions of the State and disperse political power in different arms of government. And it will set out some fundamental rights in a broad and formal way. In the everyday lives of citizens, however, these arrangements, despite being pivotal in a background sense, have little bearing. The more mundane matters are much more pressing: whether the local and national economy provides good employment opportunities; whether Special

Needs Assistants are available in schools; whether the public transport system is efficient and caters equitably for citizens living in less populated areas; whether a single mother has enough social support to care for her children.

These kinds of concerns are the essence of politics. Indeed, the fundamental rights enshrined in a constitutional text are quintessentially political claims. Although we may think of disputes concerning rights as disputes to be resolved by courts, most citizens never appear before a court in their lives. If their rights are to be vindicated – their right to education or to housing, to freedom of conscience or to privacy – they will be vindicated through the political rather than through the legal domain. The point is that it would be naïve to think that a new constitutional text might make any profound difference in the lives of citizens. What matters much more, it would seem, is our way of doing politics.

There is an important connection, of course, between the Constitution and our way of doing politics. The Irish Constitution establishes some of the most elemental aspects of our politics: the Houses of Parliament, the electoral system based on proportional representation, the model of government and more. Indeed, as this book is concerned with a Constitution for a new 'republic', there is much in the constitutional text that suggests a *republican* way of doing politics. If we take the essence of a republic to be that no individual or institution enjoys arbitrary power, Article 6, for instance, seems to do well, as it disperses political power between the three arms of government: legislative, executive and judicial. No arm enjoys absolute power. In terms of checking the power of the government, Article 15.2.1 seems also to do well, as it provides that 'the sole and exclusive power of making laws for the State is … vested in the Oireachtas.' The government may enjoy the constitutional authority to run the country, but the lawmaking power is reserved for the people's directly elected representatives, the parliamentarians. Best of all is Article 28.4.1, which holds that 'the Government shall be responsible to Dáil Éireann.' In the Irish text, the language perhaps better captures the essential principle: '*Tá an Rialtas freagrach do Dháil Éireann.*' The government is *answerable* to Dáil Éireann. Our rulers do not enjoy unaccountable power: they must answer to the people's representatives for how they exercise their power.

This essay looks at the relationship between our Constitution and our politics. It does so with an eye on republican ideals: accountability and open government, civic virtue and the common good, democracy and popular sovereignty. There are certain familiar credentials of a republican politics. It must be, for example, that our political representatives consider public policy with the commonweal in mind. It cannot be that they are moved by factional concerns: the good of the party, for instance, or of a particular interest group that supports their party. Relatedly, it cannot be that we the citizens vote for candidates based on factional or self-oriented concerns: that a particular candidate may have done us, or our locality, a good turn, or that we might deem a candidate best equipped to 'fight our corner up in Dublin.'

Rather than addressing our politics generally, however, this essay takes a specific focus. It addresses the relationship between the executive and the Parliament. For this aspect of our politics to be republican, the Parliament, as well as being a genuinely deliberative forum, must function as a meaningful check on governmental power. Government ministers really must be answerable to the people's representatives for how they run the departments of State. It cannot be that ministers are answerable to Parliament in theory, or merely in the constitutional text. They must be so answerable all of the time, as the usually monotonous life of the country's politics unfolds.

Before addressing how this relationship between government and Parliament functions in practice, it should be instructive to look at some important historical developments in the model of government established by the Irish Constitution: the Westminster model of government.

The Constitutional Authority of Parliament: Important Historical Developments

Although it is usually overlooked, and can barely be thought of as a 'Constitution' in the general sense, the Dáil Éireann Constitution of 1919 was highly significant in one respect: it established the Westminster model of responsible government in the Irish State. Article 2 (c) vested executive power in the 'Ministry' – or, in colloquial terms, the Cabinet – which was to consist of a president and four executive officers. Each member of the Cabinet was to be a member of the Dáil, to which the Cabinet was to be 'at all times responsible …'.[106] In those simple words the die was cast. In this 'constitutional moment' the model of government for Ireland was set, and it has remained so ever since.

The most distinctive feature of this model of government is, as Walter Bagehot put it in the nineteenth century, the 'close union, the nearly complete fusion of executive and legislative powers.'[107] That is, the members of the executive (or government, or Cabinet) are drawn from and chosen by members of the legislature. They are, at once, legislators and governors. They are not directly elected by the people, but are chosen by the parliamentarians. This contrasts with the presidential model of government, familiar from the United States, where the President is elected directly by the people and does not sit in the legislature. He appoints a Cabinet comprising individuals who, similarly, do not sit in Congress. It would seem that the separation of powers is more entrenched and clear-cut in the presidential model. The legislators are more independent and distinct from the government. They are more self-consciously legislators, and are likely to understand their primary role to be to make law. Parliamentarians in the Westminster model, on the other hand, are more likely to understand their primary role to be either to support or to oppose the government of the day.

A related feature of the Westminster model – and one that bears heavily on the arguments made in the pages that follow – is the party system of government, in which parliamentarians vote and generally operate as part of a cohesive parliamentary group. The emergence of the party system in the nineteenth century is generally attributed to the confluence of two factors.[108] First, the dramatic extension of the electorate in that period, which in Britain came with the passage of the Reform Acts of 1832 and 1867, meant that individual politicians could less easily deploy patronage to win elections. The larger electorate prompted the need for politicking and electioneering, which in turn meant reliance on organised party machines.[109] The second factor is more striking in the context of the modern relationship between Government and Parliament. It relates to the definitive conclusion, in 1841, of a gradual shift in one of the more important conventions of the UK Constitution, sometimes referred to as the 'Doctrine of responsible government'.[110] Since 1841, the Convention requires that a prime minister who has lost the confidence of the House of Commons no longer has the constitutional authority to govern and so must resign. Previously, the Crown could (or did) appoint a prime minister who did not enjoy the confidence of the House of Commons, or could dismiss one who did enjoy such confidence.[111]

This shift was, needless to say, an important democratic and republican advance. It empowered Parliament, and further weakened the constitutional authority of the Crown. But, as Parliament gained constitutional authority in a formal sense, it was arguably weakened in actuality. The shift placed an apparent contradiction at the heart of the Westminster model of government, and one that may still be seen to bedevil the system as it operates today, including in Ireland. The contradiction is as follows: the control and accountability of ministers came to rely on parliamentarians, a majority of whom, almost by definition, regarded their primary parliamentary function to be maintaining in power the government of the day. The function of maintaining the government of the day in power is almost the very opposite of holding the government of the day to account. Previously, under the constitutional arrangement whereby the authority of the Prime Minister rested on the goodwill of the Crown rather than on the confidence of Parliament, parliamentarians could harangue government ministers and intensively hold them to account. In other words, they could freely execute their essential function. Subsequently, the ultimate authority of the government rested on the parliamentarians themselves. If they were to remove the authority of the Prime Minister, they would themselves, very possibly, lose their parliamentary seats in a subsequent election, or at least have to go to a great deal of expense and inconvenience to retain their seats. Aside from sheer self-interest, parliamentarians would naturally be concerned to avoid the too-regular collapse of the government.[112] All of this made disciplined parliamentary parties inevitable, with government backbenchers loyal to their colleagues in Cabinet. More to the point, it weakened Parliament, causing the concentration of power and the problem of executive dominance.

Following these developments, the Westminster model came to be associated with party government and the diminution of Parliament. Lord Hailsham famously described it as an 'elective dictatorship' in his 1976 Richard Dimbleby Lecture. These shortcomings had troubled some of the leading political actors around the foundation of the Irish State. In 1919, for instance, J. J. Walsh brought a motion before the Dáil proposing a model of government more closely approximating to that of the United States, although the motion was resoundingly defeated.[113]

Similarly, the Minister for Home Affairs, Kevin O'Higgins, emphasised the shortcomings of the Westminster model in very strong language in the debates around the Free State Constitution in 1922. In defending the innovative extern minister concept, which was aimed in part at counteracting the executive dominance problem, O'Higgins insisted that 'there is nothing admirable in the Party system of Government … there is much that is evil and open to criticism' and that the various proposals in the Free State Constitution would result in 'a better system of government than that system by which men constantly, as a matter of routine, vote against their own judgement, and almost against their own conscience, for fear of bringing down the particular Party Government to which they adhere.'[114]

Despite these concerns, and despite the provisions aimed at counteracting the shortcomings of the Westminster model (those relating to the electoral system of proportional representation, for example, and to the extern minister concept), the Free State Constitution entrenched the essentials of responsible government, with an effective fusion of executive and legislative power and a government enjoying immense powers over the Dáil.[115] When de Valera came to dismantle that Constitution in the 1930s, and to pave the way for the 1937 Constitution, he was not moved by these kinds of concerns at all.[116] In fact, a system in which power was concentrated suited him quite well, as he enjoyed faithful support amongst members of a powerful and growing political movement.[117] The arrangements served him quite well in the years that followed, as he exercised an immense influence on Irish political life, as well as on Irish society more generally.

Section II | The 1937 Constitution and Tensions Between Theory and Practice

The functions of Parliament under the 1937 Constitution, just as in the case of all parliaments operating on the Westminster model, are essentially threefold: to appoint and dismiss governments, to make laws and to hold the government to account. Because of the essential contradiction referred to earlier – whereby a majority of parliamentarians regard it as their primary role to hold the government of the day in power – there is a fundamental discord between how the Dáil is to execute these functions in theory and how it actually executes them in practice. More to the point, this discord not only undermines the constitutional authority of Parliament and the republican credentials of the 1937 Constitution, it undermines the freedom of citizens, where that freedom is understood in the republican way: in terms of resilient protection, through law, from arbitrary power.

The three functions might be taken in order of ascending concern. The least troubling is the role of the Dáil in the appointment and dismissal of the government. The constitutional text envisages the Dáil as the pivotal agent in these processes. Article 13.1.1 provides that the '... President shall, on the nomination of Dáil Éireann, appoint the Taoiseach ...' while Article 13.1.2 provides that the '... President shall, on the nomination of the Taoiseach with the previous approval of Dáil Éireann, appoint the other members of the Government.'[118] Generally, a particular proposed coalition (operating on the basis of the party system) wins a majority of seats. The parliamentarians duly vote accordingly in a vote for Taoiseach and in approving his proposed members of the Cabinet.[119] The parliamentarians do not act independently: their vote is pre-ordained and can mostly be taken for granted.

Similarly with respect to Article 28.10, which is the Irish (and textual) version of the important UK constitutional convention mentioned earlier. It provides that the '… Taoiseach shall resign from office upon ceasing to retain the support of a majority of Dáil Éireann …'. Because of the solidity of political parties within the political culture, generally a government will either last a full term, or will choose to 'go to the people' at whatever time the leaders of a government and their advisors deem it most advantageous electorally. Government back-benchers will toe the line because voting against the government on a motion of confidence (or indeed, on any vote against the government line) would result in loss of the party whip. Even if the whip were ever to be regained, the earlier lack of loyalty would likely end the prospect of ever being appointed to high political office.

The weakness of Parliament in these respects is perhaps the least troubling example of the discord between constitutional theory and institutional practice. There is, after all, a clear democratic connection between the citizens and their government. The citizens elect the parliamentarians, who in turn appoint the government that has 'won' the election. In any case, a system of 166 atomised parliamentarians, or even one with only casual ties amongst them, would be chaotic and unworkable. Governments would be made and broken much too regularly, and usually, no doubt, on the basis of populist and unworthy reasons.

The difficulty, however, is that although the citizens elect their preferred government at election time, they have virtually no control over the continuance or discontinuance in office of their government in between elections. One of the outstanding theoretical features of the notion of responsible government is that the government is perpetually concerned about the prospect of being dismissed by Parliament. The thought is that the government will accordingly operate in ways that track the people's interests at all times. In practice, just as in Westminster, governments in Ireland are barely concerned at all about the prospect of being dismissed by Parliament on a month-to-month or even year-to-year basis.[120] They are concerned about their popularity amongst the electorate, certainly, with an eye on the next election (and that is not insignificant in the context of tracking the people's interest during the course of a term of government), but they are not concerned about the prospect of being dismissed in the meantime, and so, during its 'reign', a government is controlled by Parliament only in theory.

This discord is similarly evident in regard to the law-making function.[121] In this regard, it is clear that while the government of the day should not enjoy untrammelled power, neither should it be prevented from pursuing its legislative agenda. That agenda has, after all, won the approval of the citizens in a general election. Indeed, it is safe to assume that in a system that facilitates 'legislative gridlock', reforms aimed at promoting the common good would often be thwarted.

But this should not be taken to mean that the law-making role of Parliament is unimportant. The role of the government, after all, is to govern, in the sense of running the departments of State (or, in the colloquial phrase, 'running the country'). The role of making law, on the other hand, is assigned to the parliamentarians. Article 15.2.1 of the Constitution could hardly be more emphatic: the Oireachtas (or Parliament) enjoys the 'sole and exclusive' lawmaking authority. The function of parliamentarians, therefore, is to engage in the painstaking task of deliberating upon and scrutinising legislation.

An example may be instructive. Suppose a general equality bill were being introduced, and the question of appropriate exemptions from non-discrimination law were being considered. One quandary amongst many would be whether there should be an exemption to allow religious schools to discriminate against students from outside of the particular faith community. If such an exemption were justified, how far should it extend? How might such an exemption operate in practice, bearing in mind the distribution of schools across the country? Might it end up causing religious discrimination rather than promoting religious freedom? These questions – and other less exciting ones – are the essence of politics and of the parliamentary function. Very often they bring out the most fundamental disagreements in a given political community. Legislative reform, accordingly, requires very measured consideration and deliberation in various parliamentary phases in which all of the people's representatives have a meaningful deliberative role. Given the complexity of most areas of reform in the modern political world, the process should include a specialist legislative committee phase in which parliamentarians could draw on expertise, research and other resources. (On this point, the excellent deliberative process that took place in January 2013 in the Oireachtas Joint Committee on Health and Children on the question of legislation on abortion is to be applauded. This was parliamentary politics at its best. It prompts the question, however, as to why this was such an exception and not normal parliamentary procedure.)

And yet Article 15.2.1 might be described as the single greatest myth of the Constitution.[122] The government dominates to an extent that renders Parliament barely relevant. When a government minister wishes to introduce new law, they bring a 'memorandum for government' to the Cabinet, outlining the essentials of the proposed law. [123] Essentially, once they have the approval of their colleagues in Cabinet, the bill will become law, more or less in the same form. It goes through a number of formal 'stages', but the grip of the governing parties is such that, notwithstanding the power of the courts to invalidate laws that are deemed unconstitutional, the legislative outcome will essentially accord with the Minister's tastes. The legislation goes through the Office of the Parliamentary Draftsman to the Oireachtas, and then through five stages. The second and third stages are the most significant, but only in a comparative sense. The second stage is the debate on the broad principles of the bill. Although the Constitution might envisage this as the great event in the life cycle of the law (i.e., the Dáil exercising the power that it enjoys solely and exclusively), it is all a formality. The Minister reads out a script, the opposition reacts, and the bill is passed. There is little point in the opposition reacting positively by offering an alternative approach, as there is virtually no prospect that government backbenchers will breach the code of loyalty out of political conviction, placing their own political careers in jeopardy. The third is the 'committee stage'. Critically, once the bill has passed through the second stage, the relevant committee cannot amend the essential principles. In other words, the committees are left to tease out minor amendments and technical details, utterly undermining the committee concept and process.

This brings us to the most troubling discord of all. The British scholar Adam Tomkins describes the fact that the government is required to secure the support of a majority in Parliament 'every single day' in respect of 'all of its policies, decisions and actions' as 'what is beautiful about the British Constitution.'[124] He emphasises that 'Parliament is the institution that controls the government's purse strings … [and] the institution that will continuously inquire into the expenditure, administration and policy of every government department.'[125] He suggests that other constitutional states leave much of the critical task of accountability to legal controls and to bodies such as courts. The British Constitution is distinctive because it places this task in the hands of the great political institution: Parliament. The 'beauty' of this lies simply in the deeper legitimacy of that political body by comparison with legal bodies: 'no matter how democracy is defined, judges can never hope to match the democratic legitimacy of elected politicians.'[126]

The argument may be presented in an unduly optimistic way. The problem of executive dominance may not be as severe at Westminster. For one thing, there are many more MPs at Westminster than there are TDs in the Dáil. Where almost all TDs – certainly in the bigger parties – have a realistic ambition of becoming at least a junior minister at some stage in their careers, many MPs at Westminster have little or no such prospect, and see themselves as parliamentarians rather than as agents holding up or opposing a government in the hope of some day being appointed as a member of the Cabinet. There is thus a better parliamentary culture, as illustrated by the more frequent backbench revolts. But Westminster operates on the same model, and so there is a tendency towards the concentration of power in the leaders of the government.

Tomkins' more general point is nonetheless compelling: there is something beautiful about the idea that democratically elected representatives would hold our rulers to account on a day-by-day and week-by-week basis. There is something fundamentally democratic about that idea, as the voice of each citizen counts on an equal basis in electing parliamentarians. There is also something fundamentally republican about the idea. How better to hold power to account – and we should recall that the essence of republicanism is the idea that no individual or institution enjoys arbitrary power – than through representatives who have been elected in an election in which each citizen has had an equal voice? Leaving the task to bodies such as courts seems much less democratic and much less republican. Most citizens would never dream of taking a legal action to contest a particular decision by the government or by an agency of the state. Aside from the inconvenience and problems around standing, for example, such a course is simply too expensive for most citizens.

On this pivotal matter of accountability, Article 28.4.1 of the 1937 Constitution could not be more succinct: it provides only that '[t]he government shall be responsible to Dáil Éireann.' Again, however, there is discord between theory and practice. There are two systems established by the Dáil standing orders for the purpose of the holding government to account: the system of Parliamentary Questions (PQs) and the committee system.[127] The scholarship on PQs points overwhelmingly to a dysfunctional system.[128] It suggests that there is an essential culture amongst both ministers and senior civil servants of secrecy and obfuscation. The findings of the Beef Tribunal, for instance, capture the problem starkly. Mr Justice Hamilton's report suggests that if questions had been answered in the Dáil as comprehensively as they had been in the Tribunal, the Tribunal – which lasted three years and cost in excess of £17 million in the pre-Celtic Tiger era – would never have been necessary.[129] The report found evidence of deliberate vagueness and a culture of evasiveness amongst civil servants, whose primary concern was to protect their minister and department.[130] On the other side, there is evidence of an excessive tendency amongst TDs to submit PQs relating to constituency-specific issues.[131] Very often, the purpose seems to be to generate a press release for the local newspaper proclaiming the fact that they had secured some grant or social welfare payment that had already been legally available without any input from the particular TD.[132]

The weaknesses in the committee system are even more troubling. Since 1992, the committees in the Irish Parliament are structured to match or 'mark' government departments. Each committee monitors a government department, discusses its estimates, and deals with the third stage of legislation that has been introduced by the relevant minister (although, as we have seen, the fact that the committee stage comes after the stage dealing with the principles of the legislation undermines the value of specialist committees). Michael Gallagher attributes the shortcomings in the committee system to the fact that government ministers, just like all power wielders, tend to dislike scrutiny, and so have a plain disincentive to improve the system.[133] He suggests that those most likely to benefit from a strong committee system – backbenchers and the opposition – have a related disincentive: they aim to be ministers themselves some day, and would prefer not to place their future selves under a heavier burden should they be successful.

The outstanding problem in the committee system is the fact that the composition of committees, or, at least, the process of the appointment of members and of chairs, is controlled by the Cabinet. To return to what might be deemed the elementary argument, it is absurd that those who are to be scrutinised control those who are to do the scrutinising. Of the thirteen substantive committees in the present Dáil, the government parties together hold twenty-four of the twenty-six chair and vice-chair positions, with the chair of the Public Accounts Committee (as per the same constitutional convention that operates at Westminster) and the chair of the newly formed Public Service

Oversight and Petitions Committee (as promised in the Programme for Government) held by members of the opposition.[134] This amounts to a 92% share for the government parties, compared to their 68% share of the overall seats in the Dáil. Each committee also has two 'convenors', whose task it is to ensure that a quorum is present for each meeting, but who essentially act as whips ensuring voting along party lines, which, given the fact that the government tends to hold a majority on each committee, entirely emasculates the system.[135]

So we may say that although it would be beautiful if Parliament were to hold government to account in the exercise of its power – and although the constitutional text may envisage that being the case – the reality is quite different. The power of the government, once again, is virtually uncontrolled, or at least it is controlled to far less a degree than a republican Constitution would seem to require.

Conclusion

This essay has aimed to identify certain weaknesses in the Irish constitutional order. It has drawn on republican ideals in making the arguments. For citizens to enjoy freedom requires that they are resiliently protected, on an equal basis, from arbitrary or unaccountable power. Otherwise, the relationship between political power wielders and citizens is more akin to that of the relationship between a totalitarian ruler and his subjects or, in the extreme, between a master and his slave. This is not to suggest that these images accurately portray the plight of Irish citizens.

The argument is milder than that: it is that a truly republican order would involve much more in the way of the holding of power to account than the present institutional arrangements provide.

The task of reform is immense. It is one for scholars and journalists, activists and politicians and, ultimately, for all citizens. It is not possible in this essay to make any comprehensive proposals. Suffice it to say that it would seem excessive to dismiss the Westminster model of government as incapable of matching up to republican ideals. After all, that model is concerned fundamentally with the accountability and answerability of government. It is its practical operation that is problematic. No doubt there are certain surface reforms that might be worth considering, such as the previously mentioned extern minister idea.[136] So too, for example, might the recently implemented reforms to the committee system at Westminster, whereby committees are no longer controlled by the government of the day but by Parliament.[137] Similarly, an electoral system in which candidates from the same party compete within the same constituency seems to make clientelism and parish-pump politics inevitable.

Above all though, the solutions seem to lie in the general political culture. No model of government can work in the absence of a community of citizens committed to the polity and to the common good. Citizens cannot cynically dismiss politicians and the political domain and expect good political outcomes. They cannot vote for candidates who appeal to their more base 'what's-in-it-for-me' instincts and at the same time expect a political class committed to the commonweal.

There is one final point. It would seem that there is little point in writing a new constitutional text in the hope of prompting a new social and political age. The debate around a new Constitution might be helpful in encouraging debate on the political institutions and how they work. But there is much in the current Constitution that would seem to do very well on the essential themes that would inevitably emerge from such a debate: themes such as accountability, civic virtue, democracy and open government. It is just that the constitutional provisions are either entirely ignored or not taken sufficiently seriously.

A New Constitution for a New Republic

Eoin Ó Broin

Introduction

I have never been an enthusiastic supporter of the 1937 Constitution. Part of my discomfort with the document is to be found in its content. While more liberal than some of its critics suggest, it nonetheless represents a set of values that are very much out of step with both my own world view and that, I believe, of Ireland in the twenty-first century.

But my real concern with the Constitution is not so much because of the things it says, or the things it doesn't say. My problem with the text is more a reflection of my lack of enthusiasm for the State from which it emerged, and which it continues to perpetuate.

The Constitution, like the State it enunciates, is not republican. Not only is the word absent from the document, both text and State in their living form fail to meet even the most cursory definition of a republic.

A republic is a society in which the people are truly sovereign and the institutions of the State are wielded in accordance with the principles of liberty, equality and solidarity. Against this measure, clearly the 1937 Constitution and the State that accompanies it are far from republican.

Indeed, measured against the republican claims made by the founding figures of the State, laid out in the 1916 Proclamation, the Democratic Programme of the First Dáil or the Declaration of Independence, the Constitution and the State can only be considered to have failed.

As we approach the centenary of the 1916 declaration of the Republic, how will our first hundred years be remembered?

Therc is little doubt that, notwithstanding considerable achievements, the dominant themes of that history will be partition, division, conflict, poverty, inequality and the gradual erosion of popular sovereignty by political elites acting in the interests of the powerful.

The 1937 Constitution and the State it encoded into law have failed. The collapse of the banking system in 2008 and the transfer of our economic sovereignty to the Troika in 2010 were the final acts in a drama that has been many decades in the making. That failure has led to a crisis of legitimacy in the political system that governs the State; in the socio-economic model of development that dominates the State; and in the legal and constitutional framework through which the State operates. This crisis provides us with a historic opportunity to rethink and refound our claim to be a republic; to step back and take stock of the State over the past hundred years in order to learn from the mistakes and failures of that past.

In the opinion of this author, it is time to build a new republic, and as part of that process write a new republican Constitution.

Declaring my Hand

What that new republic and its Constitution might look like very much depends on two things: the values upon which we operate, and the vision we hold for Ireland's future.

Who are the people whom we intend should be sovereign? What rules should we use to govern? How should we organise our society and economy? These are the fundamental questions whose answers must underpin any meaningful revision of our Constitution and the republic it envisages.

My own answers to these questions are determined in part by ideology and in part by practical necessity. As a nationalist, I define 'the people' as all of those who live on or come from the island of Ireland; those of us born here, those who have come to live and work here and those who, for whatever reason, have gone to live abroad. Any State or republic must have a political subject. For 'a people' to be sovereign there must first be a 'people', a 'we' in whose name a Constitution is written, from whom it secures legitimacy, and for whom its laws and institutions operate.

As a republican, I argue that the rules through which we should govern ourselves as a sovereign people should be democratic, participative and empowering. Representative democracy, separation of powers and a rights-based system of law is not enough. Every citizen must have the opportunity and means to actively participate in the decision-making processes that affect their lives.

As a socialist, I believe that society and economy should be organised on the basis of equality and solidarity; that the wealth of the nation in all its forms belongs to the people of the nation and that the role of the State is to ensure equality of opportunity and condition for all. While the means and mechanisms for achieving this equality are open and subject to revision and change, the basic principle remains constant.

At a much more basic level I am a citizen and I want to lead a better life and to contribute in some small way to the improvement of life for all.

These are the values upon which I imagine the form and content of any new republic, and with it the new Constitution for that republic.

Constitutional Convention

When Fine Gael and Labour took office in March 2011, there was a widespread hope that things would change for the better. Fourteen years of corrupt and inept Fianna Fáil rule had done immeasurable damage to our economy and society, to people's faith in politics and to people themselves.

Even those of us who did not support the new Coalition had a desire to see the modest reform proposals set out in the Programme for Government achieved.

The sections on political reform seemed to hold some promise. There was talk of 'comprehensive constitutional reform.' 'The right of citizens to participate' was assured. And, we were told, 'Ireland will be transformed.'

Yet like so much of what transpired, the Constitutional Convention proposals published by government almost a year later on 28 February 2012 lacked ambition, and fell far short of the promises contained in the Programme. Instead of citizen participation we were given a glorified focus group, dominated by political parties. Gone was the promise of a 'democratic revolution', replaced with a narrowly defined agenda and with no guarantee that the government would even accept the outcome of the Convention.

The government's lack of responsiveness was confirmed on 7 June 2012, when they published their reply to a consultation on the initial proposals. There was little evidence of a willingness to listen to criticism, or to amend their original proposals in response to the views of others.

The change on offer was limited to amending specific sections of the Constitution rather than the promised wider review. While I do not discount the value of the individual changes that may emerge from the Convention process, Fine Gael and Labour had failed to live up to their initial proposition. Like so many other policy areas, it appears that the combined forces of a conservative Fine Gael and an inert civil service have conspired to neutralise and capture what was clearly a Labour-driven agenda for more far-reaching constitutional reform.

Real Constitutional Reform

The failure of the government to keep its word on the Constitutional Convention is not just yet another broken pre-election promise. We are at risk of losing a historic opportunity for change, not only constitutional but political and economic as well. The irony is that there has never been a better time for such change to be considered. Events of recent years have created both the climate and the need for such change.

The Belfast Agreement, signed in 1998, is not only about replacing the dynamics of armed conflict with those of normative political contestation, it provides for a reassessment and reconfiguration of the social, economic, political and constitutional relationships between the two States on the island.

The collapse of the Celtic Tiger has exposed the inability of neo-liberal economics to provide a sustainable and equitable model for social and economic development. While the aftershock of austerity continues to dominate government policy, its legitimacy continues to wane, and a space is opening up for the consideration of new social and economic models.

Meanwhile, across the European Union the accelerated political and economic integration of the 1980s and 1990s has given way to an institutional and existential crisis. The growing democratic deficit, the inequalities and insecurities arising from the neo-liberal capture of the social-market economy, the crisis of the Eurozone, all these have left the myths of an 'ever-closer Europe' badly exposed. Public confidence in the EU institutions is at an all-time low, and an increasingly critical engagement with the Union is gaining strength.

These interrelated realities present us with both profound challenges and exciting opportunities. For those of us living in the southern State, the socio-economic and political foundations of our recent history are being called into question; the logics of partition and anti-nationalism, aggressive economic liberalism, rising inequality, uncritical Europeanism and accelerated integration are all in crisis.

Faced with these realities, we have two clear choices. We can underestimate the extent of the crisis in which we are living and drift aimlessly through the uncharted waters that lie ahead, allowing someone else – the ECB, the European Commission or the IMF – to determine the course we chart, or we can grasp the fluidity of our current moment and actively try to shape our own future. We can consciously decide to learn from the example of others, such as the people of Iceland, who, faced with many of the same difficulties as we have faced, chose to draw a line in the sand and say: enough is enough, from today we are taking control of our own destinies.

If we choose this path, then as our first step we must start to redefine who we are; the type of society we want to build; and the constitutional and institutional architecture that will empower us to achieve that vision. This is what a Constitutional Convention should aim to achieve, not limited, piecemeal reform, but deep reflection with the potential for profound transformation.

I believe that it is a political imperative in the present moment that we should embark on an urgent debate to determine what form this thoroughgoing Constitutional Convention should take, what questions it should consider and what its remit should be.

The Process

If such a Constitutional Convention is our intention, then we need to understand that the process is as important as the content. This is why the government's proposed Convention is such a disappointment. It is designed to limit the possibility of change. It is set up not to do the very thing that is promised.

In its place we must insist on a truly national conversation about who we are as a nation, where we are going and how we are going to get there. Such a conversation must include everyone, not just a random sample of the population – as if our constitutional future could or should be determined by a professional polling company.

This will require providing all people – citizens, residents and those without status – with both the opportunity and the means to participate in this conversation. Particular attention and support will need to be provided to ensure those traditionally excluded from public debate have a real opportunity to contribute.

There can be no limits to participation. Our conversation must be truly national, accommodating the diversity of voices from all parts of the island, and it must be international, allowing contributions from the Diaspora. It must also be fully public, transparent and accountable. There must be no attempt to dominate the conversation, by political parties, by lobby groups or by experts. We must all contribute, but those of us more accustomed to such debates must demonstrate our ability to listen to and learn from others.

There must be no limits on what can be considered, no predetermined agenda, no exclusion of topics. There must be adequate time and resourcing allocated. And there must be a commitment from the government at the very outset that the conclusions will be put to the people.

A vast body of experience and literature already exists on such conversations. Organisations such as Amnesty

International and the Irish Council of Civil Liberties, to name just two, have already outlined how many of these objectives could be achieved in terms of practical proposals and structures.

This is the real value of a Constitutional Convention, if designed as a national conversation in accord with the outline above. Not only would it provide us with the opportunity to renew and redraft our Constitution as a legal basis for our society, but in doing so it would allow us to have a much deeper and more substantive conversation about that society, where it has come from, where it is today and where it wants to go tomorrow.

As always, the key question is not whether such a national conversation could be organised, but whether the political will exists to organise it.

The Content

During a recent conversation with a long-standing equality activist I asked what he thought was lacking in our current public debate. His answer was 'ambition'. My friend argued that for a variety of reasons those of us advocating substantive social, economic, political and constitutional change had been forced to lower our horizons, to focus on small, piecemeal goals, and as a result had lost our sense of what was really possible. More than anything else, my friend argued that we needed to rekindle a sense of ambition, to outline an ambitious vision of our future based on radical republican values.

But what does it mean to say we want to build a better Ireland, one based on the republican values of liberty, equality and solidarity? Are these principles not already enshrined in our Constitution, treaties and laws? Do our mainstream political parties not already claim to be motivated by these sentiments?

The stark reality of Ireland, as we approach the centenary of our founding modern moment, is that despite the rhetorical commitment of many political and social actors to these core values, the daily reality of people's lives is governed by their opposite – domination, inequality and anomie.

Some critics would argue that this is because the commitment of those mainstream political and social actors to republican values is insincere, deployed only to mask policies that promote and protect the welfare and well-being of the few at the expense of the many. Others would argue that the rhetorical adherence to these values is not matched by actions and interventions that allow for their full realisation.

Both of these arguments are correct. But there is also a deeper problem. Our conceptualisation of these values is often too narrow, too passive and too negative – limiting their true potential, and in turn constraining those actors whose commitment is honest and whose actions are well intended.

If we are to design and implement a programme of economic, social, political and constitutional change successfully, the purpose of which is to give men and women the chance of living a bigger and better life, to be truly great in whatever field of endeavour they are involved, then we must have a clear understanding of the meanings and implications of the values upon which that programme is based.

Liberty, the right of people, as individuals, communities and nations to determine their own future, was the driving force of the democratic movements of the late eighteenth and early nineteenth centuries. It challenged the right of religious and political leaders to dominate, and sought to empower people to become their own masters, to realise their individual and collective potential and to build a better world.

Throughout the nineteenth and twentieth centuries, this expansive idea of liberty as self-determination was increasingly limited to a more narrow, liberal conception of the right of individuals to live free of interference from others. The horizon of liberty was lowered – the realisation of individual liberty was increasingly pitted against constraints imposed by the collective, and in turn the function of government changed from being a promoter of self-determination to a guarantor of non-interference.

There is a need to return to the original, expansive conception of liberty as self-determination through which all people are empowered to realise their full potential.

Equality, the belief that all people are born equal and deserving of equal opportunity and outcome, presented a more profound challenge to the social and political order of the eighteenth and nineteenth centuries. From its outset, the concept was contested. There were those who sought to restrict it to a purely political and legal right, guaranteeing equal protection under the law and equal participation in decision-making, primarily through universal suffrage. There were other, more radical, voices that sought to extend the logic of equality to the social and economic spheres, demanding both an end to economic privilege and government action to redress the imbalances of poverty and inequality.

That these two dimensions of equality were interdependent – political and legal equality require social and economic equality if the terms are to have meaning – did not prevent late nineteenth and early twentieth century liberal societies from restricting the right to a purely political and legal domain. In so doing, they provided people with procedural rights that would prove unobtainable in the absence of the social and economic means to access them.

There is a need to assert the more profound meaning of equality, to extend beyond the political and into the social and economic spheres, and beyond equality of opportunity to include equality of condition. Only in this way can the procedural dimension of equality and the promise of liberty as self-determination be realised.

Solidarity, the recognition that our identities as individuals are constituted through our relationships with others, the further recognition that we can only exist in and through the collectives of which we are a part, was to become the most troublesome of values. This was particularly the case as the promise of the republican and nationalist revolutions of the late eighteenth and early nineteenth centuries were overtaken by the logics of the industrial revolution and the demands of liberal capitalism from the late nineteenth century onwards.

Rooted in the social relations of family, solidarity not only implied interdependence but also the more profound bonds of friendship, care and love that define what it means to be human and give our humanity meaning.

Late nineteenth century liberalism sought to limit the scope of solidarity, and to relegate it in its reduced sense to a newly constructed private sphere, insulated from and untroubling to the business of government and industry. Where political or economic leaders were to engage in acts of solidarity it was always to be circumscribed by the requirements of capital – ensuring that people were never so poor as to disrupt the right to private property or the effective functioning of the market. Solidarity was to be residual – a form of State charity assisting the vulnerable in order to minimise the potential for disruption caused by the worst excesses of the market.

There is a need to wrestle the true meaning of solidarity away from the restrictions placed on it by liberal utilitarianism. In doing so, we must dispense with the false idea of solidarity as an obligation to those less fortunate and assert its true meaning as the dynamic through which as human beings we come into being, and operate in the world as individuals, communities and nations.

To these three classic republican values of liberty, equality and solidarity, we must add a fourth, namely, sustainability. For two hundred years, realising the promise of the Enlightenment and French Revolution was based on the idea that we lived in a world of unlimited resources with an endless potential for absorbing growing populations, expanding industries and the ever-increasing demand for energy and raw materials. With hindsight, we now know that much of what we call social and economic progress has come at a significant ecological cost. The slow realisation that our planet's resources are finite demands an urgent reorientation of the means through which we seek to continue on the path of social and economic progress.

In every area of public policy there is a need for consideration to be given to its impact on our ecosystem, and to reorientate our goals and actions in order to at least do less damage to our planet, at best reverse the damage done in recent decades. Ecological sustainability, and in particular energy sustainability, must become a core value in our present and future. This should not be seen as a limit on our aspirations, but rather as an opportunity of enormous proportions.

A better Ireland can only be built on the guarantee of liberty as self-determination; the promotion of social, economic, political and legal equality; the practice of solidarity that recognises that individuals can only exist in the context of collectives; and policies of sustainability that find the balance between the infinite desires of human beings and the finite resources of the planet.

Equally, these four sets of values do not operate in isolation from each other but are interdependent. The extent to which we can realise and benefit from liberty and equality will be determined both by the manner in which we construct and practise solidarity and the extent to which our actions damage or sustain the planet in which we live and breathe.

For this writer at least, these values provide a firm foundation upon which a new Constitution for a new republic could be built.

A New Republic?

In November 2011, RTÉ broadcast a three-part history of Ireland entitled *The Limits of Liberty*, written and presented by Diarmaid Ferriter. The State broadcaster billed the programme as 'the story of Irish Independence. How governments of the early decades of independence were preoccupied with one overriding issue: power. Power held by small elites in what would become one of the most centralised countries in Europe.'

The documentary was a condensed version of Ferriter's history of modern Ireland. The central narrative device for the programme was a simple question: had successive Irish governments lived up to the promise that was made by the founding figures of the nation when in 1919 the first sitting of Dáil Éireann unanimously endorsed the Democratic Programme detailing the social and economic vision on which the new independent Irish Republic was to be founded?

The Democratic Programme, drafted by both Sinn Féin and the Labour Party, took the 1916 Proclamation's vindication of 'the right of the people of Ireland to the ownership of Ireland, and to the unfettered control of Irish destinies' as its starting point, and went on to detail the social and economic meanings to be drawn from this fundamental republican principle.

The Programme asserted that 'sovereignty extends not only to all men and women of the Nation, but to all its material possessions, the Nation's soil and all its resources, all the wealth and all the wealth-producing processes within the Nation.' It also prioritised the public interest over the private, affirming 'that all right to private property must be subordinated to the public right and welfare.'

The new Republic was to be 'ruled in accordance with the principles of Liberty, Equality, and Justice for all', and was to guarantee the 'right of every citizen to an adequate share of the produce of the Nation's labour.'

The depth of the Programme's support for government intervention was remarkable, given that it was written at the high point of twentieth century laissez-faire economic thinking. The document stated that, 'It shall be the first duty of the Government of the Republic to make provision for the physical, mental and spiritual well-being of the children, to secure that no child shall suffer hunger or cold from lack of food, clothing, or shelter, but that all shall be provided with the means and facilities requisite for their proper education and training as Citizens of a Free and Gaelic Ireland.'

The economy was also to be subject to the same levels of State intervention, as the government was to have a 'duty to promote the development of the Nation's resources, to increase the productivity of its soil, to exploit its mineral deposits, peat bogs, and fisheries, its waterways and harbours, in the interests [of] and for the benefit of the Irish people.'

The final lines of the Programme committed the new government to 'seek co-operation of the Governments of other countries in determining a standard of Social and Industrial Legislation with a view to a general and lasting improvement in the conditions under which the working classes live and labour.'

The Democratic Programme outlined both the values and mechanisms through which the social and economic promise of the Republican revolution was to be delivered – not just political equality but economic and social equality too. It was a radical Left Republican manifesto, combining all that was progressive in the socialist and republican traditions of its authors.

Ferriter's narrative in *The Limits of Liberty* did not rehearse the long-standing debate on the origins and intentions of the Democratic Programme or the level of actual support for its content among the deputies of the First Dáil. Rather, he asked a very simple question: measured against these founding principles unanimously endorsed by the first ever sitting of an independent Irish Parliament, how should we judge the progress of Irish society and the efforts of Irish governments from 1919 to the present?

His conclusion was damning. The Irish State from its foundations through to its present is a society deeply marked by division, conflict and inequality. The peace process brought about an end to armed conflict, but partition remains, and continues to divide Ireland north from south and unionist from nationalist. The Celtic Tiger generated historic levels of material wealth, the impacts of which were felt throughout the island, but poverty and inequality of income, health, education and power continue to deny people the chance for a better life.

Equality authorities and human rights commissions have been established, domestic and international rights legislation has been passed, governments have reiterated their commitment to principles of equality, liberty and solidarity – and yet we continue to live in a society in which the actions of governments and the lives of the men and women they govern come nowhere close to the vision outlined in the Democratic Programme.

Ten years away from the centenary of its passing, the Programme stands as a damning indictment of the failure of Irish politics to 'establish the right of the Irish people to the ownership of Ireland' and to guarantee to all 'an adequate share of the produce of the Nation's labour.'

Ferriter was right to be indignant at the growing gap that exists between the Ireland of today and the promise of the founding figures of the Republic. He was right to be indignant with an Ireland that allows more than 100,000 children to live in consistent poverty. But the Democratic Programme should do more than provoke indignation and anger. It must be a call to action to all of the people who were born in Ireland, and who have come here to live and work, to ask whether we are going to continue to accept a society that is marked by division and inequality, or whether we are going to demand change. Not the superficial change of Enda Kenny and Eamon Gilmore's phony 'democratic revolution', but rather a profound social, economic, political, constitutional and cultural change, away from the failures of the recent past and in the direction of the radical left republican vision outlined in the Democratic Programme based on the core values of political liberty, economic equality and social solidarity.

And Finally to Europe

BBC *Newsnight* economic editor Paul Mason, in his recent account of popular protests across the globe, *Why It's Still Kicking Off Everywhere*, argues that there are striking parallels between the crisis in Europe today and the turmoil on the continent during the 1840s.

During that earlier period of our continental history, political elites undermined their own legitimacy and hegemony through a mixture of political corruption and economic mismanagement. From the chaos and crisis that ensued, two of the most important political impulses of the modern era emerged: the democratic impulse of nationalism and the egalitarian impulse of socialism.

One of the figures whose life was lived at the intersection of these two impulses was the writer, activist and Young Italy founder, Giuseppe Mazzini. His words and actions were a powerful challenge to both the authoritarianism of the ancien régime and the unrestrained individualism of the emerging bourgeois liberals.

Mazzini sought to undermine the existing European order and replace it with a political and economic system that was national and cosmopolitan, egalitarian and democratic. He sought a new political, economic and constitutional order very different to that advocated either by the conservatives defending the status quo or the liberals enchanted by the promise of individual liberty and the free hand of the market.

In Ireland, the radicalism of Young Italy found its echo in the writing and activism of Thomas Davis, Charles Gavan Duffy and Fintan Lalor and the Young Ireland movement; a moment in our political and cultural history that is as much misunderstood as it is ignored.

Today, at home and across Europe, we face problems not dissimilar to those faced by Mazzini and his generation of democratic nationalists and egalitarian socialists.

Unfortunately our collective memory has been clouded by the empty promises of economic liberalism and liberal cosmopolitanism. As we grapple with the very significant challenges in front of us we could do worse than spend some time relearning the lessons from Mazzini and his generation of radicals in order to help us navigate our way to a 21st-century republic.

The window of opportunity open in front of us will not remain open indefinitely. Once closed, it may take another century before it opens again. The question facing all of us who say we want to live in a different Ireland is whether we continue to focus on small, piecemeal goals, or whether we have the courage to lift our horizons, the ambition to imagine a better future and the political will to do something about it.

To constructively misquote the Brazilian social theorist Roberto Mangabeira Unger: the world is restless, it must not be allowed despair; we need to find a better way to fulfil the central promise of democracy, to realise people's desire for greater equality and their demand for a larger life.

Bunreacht Na hÉireann 1937: Radical Reform Or Redundant Rumination?

Donncha O'Connell

Memorialising the first President of Ireland, Douglas Hyde (An Craoibhín Aoibhinn), is an appropriate context in which to reflect critically on the Irish Constitution of 1937. Hyde's role in embedding the new Irish Constitution after 1937 was not insignificant. His willingness to accept the newly created office of president was reassuring at many levels, and not just because he was a member of the Church of Ireland. Coming from the less political tradition of Conradh na Gaeilge, he was ideally suited to the office of President, designed to operate at a level 'above politics'. Although significantly incapacitated for much of his presidency, he established that office as the benign apex of constitutional ceremony and weighty symbolism, as if in answer to the paranoid suspicions of some that the presidency might morph into a dictatorship from The Park. It is good that Douglas Hyde is still remembered as a distinguished academic and statesman of outstanding honour.

The deficit in constitutional literacy

I am from the generation of Irish people that was educated – literally – under a framed copy of the 1916 Proclamation placed so high on the classroom wall as to make it unreadable. It usually had equal billing with various forms of religious iconography that included perpetual lights that seemed to be powered by a force pre-dating rural electrification. If we had wallpaper, the pattern would have been called 'Saints, Scholars and Subversives in a Titian Glow'. The curriculum was strong on Irish, English and Maths, and very strong on Religion. To illustrate how strong it was on Religion let me use this opportunity to admit – smugly, but not bitterly – that I still cannot do 'Long Division' because I was serving Mass when we did it! Irish, English, Maths and Religion, were the four certainties, every other educational 'bonus' was fortuitous.

The one thing that we never discussed in class was the state or our relationship to the State as citizens, and I cannot recall ever seeing a copy of the Constitution. There were tangential moments of what I would call 'patriotic transfer', when we learned things like the words of The 'Foggy Dew' or 'A Nation Once Again' but they felt more like occupational therapy for the teacher and his guitar. Thus, we sang of our willingness to die for the State that we lived in and loved, but barely understood. More importantly, we sang raucously of our willingness to fight against the State that we lived beside and, ironically, in which we might eventually live.

The curriculum under which my age cohort was educated quite simply ignored and, I presume, consciously avoided the idea of political formation or constitutional literacy through education. Our consciousness of the political process might never have occurred were it not for periodic temporary evictions or 'days off' from the school to facilitate polling stations in elections. (The only other 'days off' were those sanctioned by the bishop on rare visits to the school, and those resulting from naturally occurring disasters like snow, outbreaks of contagious diseases, infestations of head lice and lightning (even if the lightning didn't affect the perpetual light)).

In the absence of a developed capacity for critical engagement with political thinking, it should hardly, therefore, come as a surprise that the ideologically indistinguishable Fianna Fáil-Fine Gael dominance of Irish politics endured for so long, and that tribal political affiliations passed through generations for as long as they did. It should be a cause of much greater concern that the permanent anchor tenants of government since 1922 have been either Fianna Fáil or Fine Gael.

That is not to say that teachers did not pass on their Civil War and other non-correlative biases in delivering the curricular goods. They most certainly did. The point I am emphasising, however, is that the curriculum 'didn't go there' when it came to what, in other countries, would have been taken for granted as civic formation, or what I call constitutional literacy through education.

In lamenting this, I am not arguing for the kind of brainwashing that occurs in other countries involving the collective recitation of oaths of fidelity and saluting flags. What I regret is that, at a critical stage in the evolution of the State, we failed to use our education system to address the question of constitutional illiteracy when it might have developed the capacity of citizens to engage critically with their State. We opted for different versions of unthinking nationalism when we might at least have opted for thinking nationalisms.

Even if this has since been addressed in curricular reform – however imperfectly and, arguably, at the expense of good education in History – the earlier neglect has an enduring adverse implication, particularly for people of my own generation.

Competing centrisms

Our political spectrum is crowded in the middle with left-wing Christian Democrats and right-wing Social Democrats all competing for ownership of a confused and, at times, incoherent Centrism. The 'party of government' has almost always been Fianna Fáil, with Fine Gael acting as its ideologically indistinguishable understudy. Of course, smaller parties have played a disproportionately important role, but the consistent pattern in Irish elections – albeit with diminishing numbers – has been that Irish people largely favour centrist parties. This pattern is confirmed if Labour is viewed as a centrist party – a debate, perhaps, for another publication.

And, yet, we remain happy to acquiesce in the mythology of the Irish as 'a politically sophisticated race'. This is nonsense. We may be politically cunning and ideologically non-committal, but we are demonstrably incapable of big political thinking or visionary politics. We are operators rather than thinkers, pragmatists who adapt and sometimes subvert political systems rather than design them, electors in an open marriage with Fianna Fáil or Fine Gael. The 'amoral localism' so well described by the late Professor Peter Mair at the 2011 MacGill Summer School defines Irish politics in a way that simply cannot be excused or explained away as a feature of politics in any small country.

Constitutional design

The story of the 1937 Constitution and its emergence from the messy dispensation that existed from 1922 illustrates this point. Although it would be churlish not to acknowledge that the drafting of the Constitution was a borderline visionary moment, its birth was also grounded in opportunism. De Valera seized the opportunity of the abdication crisis – one of those periodic British constitutional crises that erupt when the love lives of significant royals become more complicated than their unwritten Constitution can bear – to hasten the creation of a context requiring a new Irish Constitution that was, in many respects, similar to its predecessor.

There was minimal innovation, with the Cabinet or 'Executive' remaining at the centre of power – answerable, in theory, to a Dáil and a restored but weakened Seanad. The list of recognised fundamental rights was extended and Natural or 'Higher' Law language was used in various parts of the text of the Constitution. The practical consequences of including such language – which became very apparent in controversial cases in the 1960s, 1970s and 1980s – may have been unintended. De Valera's fond hopes of territorial reintegration and Irish language revival were also inserted as suspended realities. God was given more than one decent mention and, critically, popular sovereignty was made more meaningful than it had been under the previous dispensation by providing that the text of the Constitution could only be amended by popular referendum with simple majority voting. It would seem, according to Mr Justice Gerard Hogan's magisterial study on the history of the 1937 Constitution, that De Valera did intend that the explicit power of judicial review of legislation would be used and, despite concerns expressed by civil servants, that he even considered establishing a constitutional court to give greater effect to this intention.

A bare majority of the people voting in 1936 approved De Valera's Constitution, and most women voting did not. Seventy-five years later it remains the Constitution of this State – it is as enigmatic as *Ulysses*: everyone knows about its existence, but few people know anything about it.

Constitutional re-design

In criticising the 1937 Constitution and the mechanisms for its reform, I am not dismissing the work of far-seeing constitutional architects like Éamon de Valera and John Hearne, nor indeed of those, like Douglas Hyde, who helped make de Valera's Constitution work. In fact, I am seeking to promote a comparable but different visionary ambition that engages seriously with the possibilities for renewing and rebuilding the damaged Irish State by means of constitutional renewal and reform. That is not to say that the key to our salvation lies only in constitutional reform, or that blame for our current woes lies mainly in the Constitution but, rather, it is to argue for more than a merely surface-level response by way of constitutional reform supported by a deliberative process that approximates to little more than redundant rumination.

The alternative idea of a radical review of the Constitution is no academic whimsy. In February 2010, *The Irish Times* published an extended series of essays – 'Renewing the Republic' – by varied and respected commentators calling for quite fundamental reform of the Constitution as a means of renewing politics and democracy in Ireland. Political parties were not far behind.

In particular, the Labour Party leader, Eamon Gilmore TD addressing his party's annual conference in NUI Galway in April 2010, called for the establishment of a Constitutional Convention composed of experts, specialists and randomly chosen citizens, stating: 'It is time, in my view, for a fundamental review of our Constitution. There is much about the Constitution that has served us well, but it is a document written in the 1930s for the 1930s, a time when one church was considered to have a special position and women were considered to be second-class citizens. And if we are to truly learn from the experience of the last ten years, then we need to look again, in a considered way, at the fundamental rules that bind us together.'

In the General Eelection that took place in 2011, all of the main political parties, including Fianna Fáil as it exited government, put forward manifestos with ambitious plans for radical political renewal through constitutional reform. There was not even a muted defence of the status quo. Yet, no mainstream party called in unequivocal terms for a new Constitution.

The 1937 Constitution has many strengths, not all of which were apparent to its framers. It is strong on due process, or what is called, more prosaically, the right to a fair trial or fair procedures. It is admirably protective of the right to personal liberty, and makes detailed provision for habeas corpus. Its provisions on religion were surprisingly liberal for their time. It has unrealised potential in areas like human dignity and positive obligations. Its dualist position on international law would be unobjectionable but for the dualist politics that it has spawned.

It is, however, lamentably weak on equality, and offensively stereotypes women (or mothers) while ignoring fathers. On socio-economic rights it is platitudinous. Its previously mentioned invocation of Natural Law and the naturalistic fallacies that go with it could undermine its authority in a serious way, but, thankfully, that risk has been 'managed' by pragmatism on the part of most judges.

As regards politics, the 1937 Constitution preserves a strongly executive-centred polity and pays lip service to the idea of parliamentary accountability. Although its rhetoric on judicial independence is unequivocal, this is undermined by a judicial appointments process that places the executive at the heart of the action. Things that were not even mentioned in the Constitution – like neutrality and Cabinet confidentiality – have enjoyed the status of constitutional precepts anyway. Other aspirations – like territorial reintegration, language revival and female domesticity – were simply parts of De Valera's utopian future written in the present tense, describing what might be as if it was.

The amendment process

And, yet, the 1937 Constitution has stood the test of time. Without repeating the fatal flexibility of its 1922 counterpart, it has proved amenable to change. The sovereign people, who are, in constitutional terms, the arbiters of such change, have shown themselves (for the most part) to be discerning in referenda to consider constitutional amendment proposals.

Early proposals by Fianna Fáil to jettison PR-STV, the constitutionally prescribed voting system, were rightly rejected. While amendments to facilitate the ratification of EU treaty changes are usually accepted, this is not always the case, hence the references to the Nice 1 and 2 and Lisbon 1 and 2 referenda. Unbalanced and unfair amendments, like the Thirtieth Amendment of 2011 that sought to create a power of parliamentary inquiry with minimal judicial review, don't necessarily survive scrutiny by a sceptical public. Of course, there have been less edifying moments of constitutional amendment, such as the disastrous Eighth Amendment on the right to life of the unborn in 1983, the rejection of the initial proposal for divorce in 1986 and, I would contend, the citizenship referendum of 2004.

Almost all proposals for constitutional amendment emanate from the government, and all require parliamentary approval before being put to the people in a referendum. To date, the two major reviews of the Constitution that have taken place – one by an All-Party Oireachtas Committee in 1967 and the other by a government-appointed Review Group chaired by T. K. Whitaker in 1996 – have yielded virtually nothing by way of significant constitutional reform. Both reviews contained some excellent recommendations, and yet neither had impact measurable in terms of constitutional change. The Oireachtas Committee on the Constitution has also done highly creditable work, but with very little to show by way of actual constitutional reform.

The reason for this is that the government (i.e. the Executive, transient elected and permanent unelected) is the gatekeeper of the processes of constitutional reform. Governments try to be risk-averse, and constitutional referenda are risky. As so many referenda concern changes to EU treaties and related matters, it is almost certainly the case that we would have had far fewer such referenda were it not for the majority Supreme Court decision in the *Crotty* case.

In fact, it is arguable that the more fundamental and holistic changes to the 1937 Constitution have been inspired by supranational and transnational stimuli in the form of constitutional developments within the European Union and rare but important developments with constitutional implications in Anglo–Irish relations. The latter transnational dimension has always been a complicating factor in Irish constitutional affairs.

There are probably few votes in broad agendas for constitutional reform and, as certain constitutional issues can be highly divisive, most politicians view ambitious constitutional reform plans with a degree of caution as to the political hazards entailed. Garret FitzGerald was one of the few politicians in recent times with a serious mission of constitutional reform designed to make the Irish State seem less sectarian and irredentist. This was famously characterised by the late Brian Lenihan Snr. as 'a constitutional crusade'. It led, for complex reasons, to decidedly mixed results.

This was hardly surprising at the time, particularly in relation to issues like abortion and divorce. At any time except, perhaps, in the immediate aftermath of some upheaval or revolution it is, understandably, difficult to engage public opinion in the business of creating or renewing a political dispensation by means of what seem to be constitutional abstractions. There is an understandable nervousness on the part of politicians and civil servants about visionary claims rubbing up against public cynicism.

Does that mean that all the high-minded talk about political and constitutional reform in the period prior to the 2011 General Election was no more than the rhetoric of reluctant reformers; that the Constitutional Convention, which seemed so ambitious when first mentioned by Eamon Gilmore, was little more than a sop to that section of the electorate concerned about the structural dimension of State architecture contributing to the political and economic crisis?

Constitutional reform now: 'we are where we are'

Why should we expect anything from the Constitutional Convention? There are two reasons why it might have been expected to yield meaningful or even radical constitutional reform:

1. The current Fine Gael–Labour government actually has a mandate to implement a political reform agenda that requires constitutional

amendment, and arguably has a mandate for radical reform; and

2. Directly engaging the citizenry in the deliberative process of a Convention is novel in a way that previous reviews were not. It is less immediate than a referendum considering a single proposal, and could allow for some thoroughgoing and balanced reflection on the Constitution if done properly.

So why, then, am I pessimistic about the Constitutional Convention's prospects?

I am pessimistic because the Constitutional Convention, as currently envisaged, is clearly not intended to engage deeply with an agenda for real political reform. This is in marked contrast to previous reviews of the Constitution.

The 1937 Constitution has been subjected to various forms of review that usually coincide with its significant anniversaries. Thus, having reached its thirtieth birthday, it was reviewed by an All-Party Oireachtas Committee that made worthy recommendations, some of which were well ahead of their time. It was subjected to a more forensic review in 1996 by the Constitution Review Group, chaired by T. K. Whitaker, just prior to its sixtieth birthday. The report of that group spawned numerous reports by the Oireachtas Committee on the Constitution, many of which made sensible recommendations grounded in workable political consensus, but most of which were ignored. Its seventieth birthday was marked by some academic conferences, and now, on the occasion of its seventy-fifth anniversary, the Constitution is to be subjected to the scrutiny of a Constitutional Convention made up of politicians and citizens.

The Convention starts with the formidable challenge of dealing with the following items of potential constitutional reform within a tight time frame of twelve months:

- Reducing the term of the presidency to five years;
- Reducing the voting age to seventeen ;
- Same-sex marriage;
- Reviewing the Dáil electoral system;
- Blasphemy; and
- The position of women in the home.

There are also other 'fringe events' that rather dwarf the birthday celebrations represented by the establishment of the Convention – including a referendum to insert an explicit reference to children's rights in Article 42 of the Constitution – passed at the end of 2012 – as well as a referendum to abolish Seanad Éireann promised (or, more correctly, rescheduled) for late 2013. This proposal was rejected by a margin of 2% in a referendum held on 4 October 2013 in which just over 39% of those eligible to vote voted.

As if that wasn't enough, in July 2012 the Minister for Justice, Equality & Defence, Alan Shatter TD, floated the possibility of further constitutional referenda on the establishment of a Court of Civil Appeal, an enabling provision to allow for the establishment of, *inter alia*, Family Courts, various changes to the procedure whereby the President may refer legislation to the Supreme Court to test its constitutionality including, controversially, provision to allow the Supreme Court to refuse to accept such references and provision to allow the government to refer international agreements to the Supreme Court prior to ratification to ascertain – by way of an advisory opinion – their compatibility with the Constitution. Two of these proposals – to establish a Court of Civil Appeal and remove the so-called 'single judgment rule' – were approved in the referendum that also considered the Seanad abolition proposal.

Bearing in mind that five referenda have already been held in the term of the current government since it came to power in 2011, we can, presumably, expect every record of attempted constitutional amendment to be broken by this administration before it leaves office in 2016. The late Garret FitzGerald would not even have dared to dream of such a constitutional crusade!

Much of the commentary about the proposed Constitutional Convention has been negative or sceptical, and has focused on both process and substance. For some people who are keen on the idea of citizens' assemblies and deliberative democracy as a supplement to representative democracy, the inclusion of politicians in the membership of the Convention is a distortion. According to this view, a citizens' assembly should be a forum for citizens alone, although it has been argued by some that the mixture of citizens and politicians has benefits.

For others, the proposed agenda of the Convention is disappointingly narrow and shallow, and the time allowed for it to deliberate is inadequate. Issues like the voting age and the length of a presidential term are dismissed as unimportant, while other issues like same-sex marriage and the position of women in the home have already been considered in detail by other expert bodies.

There are, of course, people who are just dismissive of the whole project – people who view most deliberative processes as wasteful or pointless indulgences. While what has emerged by way of concrete proposal is a compromise between both parties in government following some consultation with Opposition parties, it falls short of the rhetorical promise held forth by Fine Gael and Labour prior to their coming into office. This is a serious matter for those who believe in political renewal by means of constitutional reform.

The Convention was not, for example, allowed to consider the highly questionable proposal to abandon bicameralism by abolishing Seanad Éireann. Nowhere on its preset agenda is there any mention of correcting the imbalance that exists as between the government and the Oireachtas, although the issue of Dáil electoral reform may afford some scope for getting at executive accountability, however tangentially. The fact that it has been given an agenda set by government is, in and of itself, an emasculation of the idea of a Citizens' Assembly, thus compounding the more fundamental dilution of the concept by the inclusion of politicians in membership of the Convention. What might have been a genuinely novel and worthwhile exercise in deliberative democracy has been compromised from the outset. In fact, we have diluted the potential for some real citizen-led, deliberative democracy by imposing an unnecessary and ill-suited layer of representative democracy. A much more imaginative and serious approach could have been taken.

An insincere and limp approach to constitutional reform, especially at a time of real anxiety about the structural defects of the State is, ultimately, damaging to the constitutional edifice that is the State and seriously undermining of the public trust that is essential to maintaining a semblance of social contract crystallised in the formal or 'constitutional' relationship of citizens to their State. This damage is all the more inexcusable when done by those who promised so much in the area of constitutional and political reform as part of a platform for achieving power.

Citizens become upset when politicians do things for which they have no mandate, but they become confused when politicians do not do things for which they have a mandate. That confusion can lead to disappointment and anger, but even if it does not, it erodes public trust. The erosion of public trust is like a decay-causing plaque, and no amount of PR 'flossing' can reverse the decay caused by the erosion of that trust. Overselling or protesting too much about the merits of the compromised Constitutional Convention simply entrenches cynicism.

Radicalism should not be confused with extremism or fundamentalism. To be radical is to address the root causes of problems. The proposed soft-focus format and agenda of the Constitutional Convention will not allow for a radical appraisal of the Irish Constitution, or of the link between our constitutional arrangements and our current woes. Such an appraisal might well yield recommendations that are far from radical, in terms of constitutional reform, but to have the possibility of a radical assessment foreclosed is deeply disappointing.

Towards a Feminist Constitution

Orla O'Connor

Introduction

In 1936, while formulating a new Constitution, Éamon de Valera established a civil service committee to assist him. They were all men. He also took extensive advice from the presidents of the Supreme Court and the High Court. Both were men. Archbishop of Dublin John Charles McQuaid also heavily influenced the final text. There were only three women TDs at the time, none of whom said a word in the Dáil debates on the draft.

Women's organisations made trenchant efforts to reset de Valera's sexist trajectory. Cork playwright and poet Kathy D'Arcy has dramatised the events in her play *This is my Constitution*. It is based solely on archive correspondence and materials from the period when the 1937 Constitution was being drafted. It shows the strength of views by women as well as the conservative approach taken by the then government. The opening gambit of the play is the voice of a woman activist: 'The death knell of the working woman is sounded in the new Constitution which Mister de Valera is shortly to put before the country. Mister de Valera is a reactionary where women are concerned. He dislikes and distrusts us as a sex. He showed his hand for the first time in the Conditions of Employment Bill, which gives him power to exclude women from any industries in which he does not need them.'[138]

De Valera yielded little: almost none of the requests made by women's organisations were met with positive answers. As Diarmaid Ferriter observes, 'Letters of protest to the Government … came from domestic and international organisations who suggested "these clauses are based on a fascist and slave conception of woman as being a non-adult person who is very weak and whose place is in the home. Ireland's fight for freedom would not have been so successful if Irish women had obeyed these clauses." Lucy Kingston, honorary secretary of the National Council of Women of Ireland, expressed her association's opposition on the grounds that the objectionable clauses were not "in keeping with the spirit of the Republican Proclamation of 1916."'[139]

The 1916 Proclamation is often viewed as the moral cornerstone of the Irish nation; its call to 'cherish all the children' has become a rallying cry for those who believe that dignity, equality and compassion are values more conducive to a holistically developed republic than material wealth or privileging the religious beliefs of one group over another. But like any political document the Proclamation was cobbled together – albeit with supreme eloquence – by a coalition, and within the coalition there were differences. In formulating the 1937 text, de Valera could draw with ease on the religious nationalism of Pearse, but rely less on the republican socialism of Connolly.

In so doing, de Valera cast his long shadow over the women of Ireland for generations to come. He designed a Constitution that was sexist, exclusive, and reductionist. It gave legal and moral force to his dreams of a Catholic Ireland where women stayed at home and served their men. There were alternatives: the radical programme of the first Dáil in 1919 contains much of the spirit of equality in its text. The values of 'liberty, equality and justice for all' were to be the pre-eminent values for the future Irish State.[140] If we wanted one, this document could also serve as a useful antecedent to draw on while formulating a new, more inclusive Constitution.

The history of Bunreacht na hÉireann is deeply significant, because the quality of the process is a good indicator of the quality of the result. If we want a Constitution for all citizens, shared and owned equally by women and men, then an open process that shifts the power away from small, appointed groups is essential. The development of a new Constitution must, firstly, be based on a process that incorporates the voice, views and value of women – in all their diversity – on an equal basis to men. Such a process tells us the kind of engagement which citizens, especially women, will have with the new text.

Today's Constitution is a function of the patriarchal society which produced it. Its values, institutions and practices – while not without worth – do not represent the kind of document over which women in Ireland feel ownership. A new Constitution should embody the spirit of participation by ensuring that women's voices play a meaningful role in the formulation and decision-making process.[141] This process could throw up a range of previously unheard of or unexplored possibilities. But we can be certain that by giving voice and power to women this document would already be the political and moral antonym of its predecessor, and so the beginning of a society over which all citizens can claim ownership.

Equality and Rights as the Cornerstone of our New, Feminist Constitution

The Constitution is our most important document: our societal blueprint. It sets out a framework that defines the functions and limitations of the State, but also of the value system that underpins our relationship, as citizens, to the State and with each other. In a research paper written for the National Women's Council of Ireland, Dr Alan Brady of Trinity College Dublin establishes that written constitutions serve broadly three different purposes: 'First, they are a symbolic statement about who we are as a nation and how we understand ourselves. Secondly, they set up the institutions of government and very importantly they decide which institution has the last say if there is a disagreement … Thirdly, a written Constitution will usually protect certain fundamental rights. We usually refer to these as "Constitutional rights" but they contain very similar ideas to the body of rights generally referred to as "human rights" and are broadly drawn from the same philosophical tradition.'

Each of these strands can, and does, have an impact on all citizens: women and men. A starting point for the National Women's Council of Ireland, and other feminists, is that our new Constitution would explicitly express the values of feminism. Feminism must inform all three components of our new text. This will be done by building the Constitution on the basis of an expanded range of human rights; a clear and justiciable expression of the desire for an equal society; and an understanding of the possibilities for development of women and men. Otherwise our choice is the 'corrosive inequality' of the past, which, as Tony Judt writes, 'rots societies from within. The impact of material differences takes a while to show up: but in due course competition for status and goods increases; people feel a growing sense of superiority (or inferiority) based on their possessions; prejudice towards those on the lower ranks of the social ladder hardens; crime spikes and the pathologies of social disadvantage become ever more marked. The legacy of unregulated wealth creation is bitter indeed ... between 1983 and 2001 mistrustfulness increased markedly in the US, the UK and Ireland – three countries in which the dogma of unregulated individual self-interest was assiduously applied to public policy.'[142]

If we are to avoid the consequences of laissez-faire approaches to social organisation then our new Constitution must expressly and explicitly be grounded in the ideals of human rights and equality by providing accountability mechanisms to ensure the development of a more equal society.

Our contemporary understanding of human rights is rooted in the tradition that developed in the aftermath of the horrors of World War Two and was codified in a variety of texts, most famously the Universal Declaration of Human Rights. The Declaration has, in turn, been further developed into a range of human rights treaties, including the Convention on the Elimination of Discrimination Against Women (CEDAW), the Convention on Civil and Political Rights and the Convention on Economic, Social and Cultural Rights.

Such fundamental rights should be clearly integrated into the new text. This should also include a mechanism that ensures swift and simple ratification of human rights treaties. Ireland has a long, unfortunate tradition of leaving extended gaps between the formal process of signing up to international human rights treaties and the final process of bringing them into legal effect on the statute books. Our new Constitution presents a real chance to close this gap.

There are two philosophies of equality that can be applied in the development of constitutional law. The first is known as processes equality, which is essentially a laissez-faire approach, and which has been the philosophy adopted by thc Irish courts in dealing with equality issues. A process equality approach asks that people be treated in an equal way and that no discrimination happen at all. The second approach is known as substantive equality, and reasons that equality of outcome, rather than of treatment, is what matters.

These two notions of equality are described as: 'Process equality imagines a level playing field and sets out to keep it level. Substantive equality says that the playing field is not level and sets out to even it out.'[143]

In a real republic we have a duty to seek equality of outcome proactively. Philip Petit names the most fundamental guarantee in a republic as freedom, which:

'... in the republican key is a rich and demanding ideal that is inconsistent with any form of subjugation ... The observation has practical implications. Under the classical liberal idea of freedom as non-interference – freedom as free rein – a woman might be as free as her husband, a servant as his master, even while enjoying little protection against their arbitrary power. Under the republican idea of freedom, as extended to women and servants, this could never be so. To be truly free the woman or the servant would have to command the respect of the husband or master on pain of legal or cultural redress, not just happen to enjoy the benefit of his kindly disposition.'[144]

Our shared Constitution must be grounded in substantive legal mechanisms that promote the freedom and equality of all citizens and protect those freedoms when under attack. In legal terms this means examining the effect of a provision to establish whether it limits the privileges of a dominant group and, significantly, enhances the privileges of more vulnerable groups.

Here, then, lies the nexus between rights and equality. Where individuals, or collections of individuals in a marginalised group, are subject to policies and practices that create or perpetuate vulnerabilities, this is where our focus should be. So while all citizens have rights, our focus for the vindication of rights through social or legal policy must be on those citizens who – for whatever reason – do not enjoy their rights to the fullest possible extent.

The UCD Equality Framework[145] can be applied to ensure that we eliminate inequality in four key spheres of women's lives:

1. The economic sphere;
2. The affective sphere;
3. The political sphere; and
4. The cultural sphere.

Valuing Work and Care

Even the most benign interpretation of Bunreacht na hÉireann's Article 41 illustrates a text that is out of step with a modern country. This benign view could argue that at least there is a recognition of the role of care, and an undertaking that mothers providing a care role will not be obliged to work outside the home. The problem with the Article is that the role is ascribed exclusively to women. So surprising is the text to a modern eye that it is worth restating Article 41.2:

1. In particular, the State recognises that by her life within the home, woman gives to the State a support without which the common good cannot be achieved.
2. The State shall, therefore, endeavour to ensure that mothers shall not be obliged by economic necessity to engage in labour to the neglect of their duties in the home.

The text is an embodiment of the idea of women as subjected to the duties decided upon by men. Its placement in the Constitution should have led to recognition of the value of the contribution women make through unpaid care work in our society. However, the text was hardly ever subjected to judicial scrutiny or use. It had little or no impact on the positive formulation of social policy or bettering the position of women. In fact it became what it was always intended to be: a shackle, not a compliment.

The UN body tasked with examining and upholding women's rights globally, the Committee for the Elimination of Discrimination Against Women (CEDAW), recognised this. They have criticised Ireland's retention of Article 41.2 in its current form. They express concern at the persistence of traditional, stereotypical views of the social roles and responsibilities of women and men in the family and in society at large. CEDAW suggests that the male-oriented language be replaced with gender-sensitive language to convey the concept of gender equality more clearly.[146]

CEDAW's view is that it is not only problematic to assign a highly restrictive role to women in Irish society, it is also highly inaccurate. Women in Ireland today play multiple roles, and are subjected to a constant balancing act between them all. In her widely circulated essay, Barack Obama's former advisor, Anne Marie Slaughter, characterised the dilemma of modern women: 'why women still can't have it all.'[147] For decades, women have increasingly participated in paid work. In 2011, 46.7% of those in employment were women,[148] and in 2012, 55% of women were in employment.[149] On top of this, the majority of unpaid care work continues to be provided by women. Our most recent Census, in 2011, indicates that 61% of carers are women,[150] 11.2% of all females aged 45–49 years act as carers,[151] and women provided almost two-thirds (66.1%) of all care hours.[152] The census question[153] did not include the unpaid care work provided to children, 86% of which is estimated to be carried out by women.[154]

There is the reality that women are far less likely to be in the labour force, and are almost 25 times more likely to be looking after home/family than men. In 2009, women's income, was around 73% of men's income and even after adjusting for the fact that men work longer hours, a woman's hourly earnings were around 94% of men's.[155] Disposable income for households headed by a male continues to be significantly higher than for households headed by a female, and deprivation rates are higher for women and households headed by a woman than men or households headed by a man.[156]

Changes to our Constitution, then, must be centred on this dilemma: how can we provide women with the freedom to make a meaningful contribution in the workplace (particularly as they are paid less), simultaneously imbuing real value into the paid and unpaid care work they do, while at the same time seeking to redistribute the responsibilities of men into the domestic sphere?

This task can be fulfilled with two clear mechanisms. Firstly, we should include a symbolic recognition of the role and value of both women and men as caregivers in Irish society. Secondly, the Constitution must provide a clear rights-based framework for the provision of basic minimum standards in the area of socio-economic rights, which would be likely to improve the position of a great many women in Ireland and to improve their economic independence.[157]

Valuing Care Work (Paid and Unpaid) by Women and Men

Care work is essential to the common good: it performs vital social and economic functions.[158] Recognition and valuing of affective care is fundamental to full equality for women. Affective care refers to human dependence and interdependence, and the right to give and receive love and care.[159] One of the key problems is that while there has been a significant increase in women's participation in the labour market, this has not been balanced by any increase in the contribution of men to domestic or care work. Nor has there been an adequate State response through recognition of, or investment in, care work.[160]

In a publication for the National Women's Council of Ireland (NWCI) and SIPTU,[161] Dr Mary Murphy argues that Ireland still has a highly gendered pattern of care and work. Ireland has moved from a male breadwinner/mother model, where there are fully gender-differentiated work and care roles. We now have two models: firstly, a mother/worker model, where women are still the primary carers, although with limited labour market roles; secondly, to a lesser degree, we have moved some way towards an adult/worker model, where both adults work and care is purchased in the marketplace. Murphy argues that Ireland now needs to move towards a carer/worker model where a care ethic is fully accommodated in the design of the labour market, both adults work less than full time and share care equally.

For real constitutional reform, the challenge is to balance the recognition of the importance of care work within any society with the reality that the majority of this work is provided by women, while not ascribing this role exclusively to women.

Rather than ascribing any particular role to either gender, the Constitution could make a strong symbolic statement on equality and on the role of affective care in the achievement of equality. An appropriate model could build on the work of the Constitutional Review Group, but go further by recognising that care work is conducted in a range of spheres, not simply in the home: 'The State recognises that home, family and community life give society a support without which the common good cannot be achieved. The State shall endeavour to support persons caring for others.'[162]

This statement would remain, however, in the realm of the symbolic. It would need to be supported by justiciable mechanisms that protect women entering the labour market in lower paid jobs and poor women's socio-economic rights.

Realising the socio-economic rights of women

Building on the recognition of care work, our new Constitution could be used to make a strong statement about socio-economic rights in Ireland. Such a change would rank among the most significant changes to improve the position of women in Irish society because these rights protect vulnerable groups including the low paid and those living in poverty.

The 1937 Constitution provided little in the way of economic and social rights. However, it did provide for free primary education for all children, and in Article 45 there are sections known as the directive principles of social policy. These principles ascribe to the State a need for an egalitarian economic and social policy. However, while the provision for free primary education has been developed by the courts (most notably in *TD v Minister for Education*[163]), the courts took a different view of the directive principles, essentially deciding that it was the prerogative of the Oireachtas to implement them. The legislature failed to respond accordingly. However, in a model that borrowed heavily from Ireland, part IV of the Indian Constitution also describes directive principles. 'Like the Irish principles, they are expressly non-enforceable by the courts. However, unlike the Irish principles, the Indian principles have been used to interpret the meaning of other rights which are enforceable. For example, in the case of *Olga Tellis v Bombay Municipal Corporation*[164] the applicants were living on the streets and in slums in Bombay. The Corporation sought to forcibly evict them and they argued that this deprived them of their livelihood, since many of them were engaged in street trading of one form or another.

The directive principles of the Indian Constitution include a right to an adequate means of livelihood. However, as the directive principles are not enforceable, the applicants could not rely on this provision. However, the Supreme Court held that the right to life must be interpreted in light of the directive principles and so interpreted the right to life as including the right to a livelihood.'

This example is a useful one to examine for a number of reasons. Firstly, it illustrates the power of the courts to set the direction of policy. This happened in the Indian case when the courts were proactive and in the Irish case by the decision of the courts not to act. Secondly, it may illustrate a constitutional model that is broadly consistent and coherent with our own traditions, but with a more radical effect. All that would be needed is for the current Constitution to be updated with an indication that the directive principles are enforceable through the courts.

However, an even more desirable model would be the South African one, which contains substantial, directly enumerated and justiciable guarantees of socio-economic rights. Sections 26 and 27 state:

> 26. Housing
> (1) Everyone has the right to have access to adequate housing.
> (2) The State must take reasonable legislative and other measures, within its available resources, to achieve the progressive realisation of this right.
> (3) No one may be evicted from their home, or have their home demolished, without an order of court made after considering all the relevant circumstances. No legislation may permit arbitrary evictions.
>
> 27. Health care, food, water and social security
> (1) Everyone has the right to have access to
> (a) health care services, including reproductive health care;
> (b) sufficient food and water; and
> (c) social security, including, if they are unable to support themselves and their dependants, appropriate social assistance.

(2) The State must take reasonable legislative and other measures, within its available resources, to achieve the progressive realisation of each of these rights.

(3) No one may be refused emergency medical treatment.[165]

Acknowledging the power of these Articles, Brady suggests that 'In leading cases, the South African Constitutional Court has interpreted these rights as requiring the government to devise and implement programmes within available resources. In *Government of the Republic of South Africa v Grootboom*[166] the court ordered that a programme be devised to provide basic shelter for a group of people who had been living in a shanty town and had subsequently been evicted from private land. In Minister for *Health v Treatment Action Campaign* the government was required to come up with a programme to give HIV medication to pregnant women to combat mother-to-child transmission of HIV.[167] In neither case did the court order the expenditure of very specific sums, but in both cases the existence of a right and a court order requiring some level or realisation was present.'[168]

Ireland's international obligations also indicate that including such a provision in our Constitution would make real sense. The International Covenant on Economic Social and Cultural Rights (ICESCR) was signed by Ireland in 1973, although only ratified in 1989. The ICESCR commits the State Parties to 'progressive realisation' to the 'maximum of available resources' of a range of rights, such as an adequate standard of living including housing,[169] enjoyment of the highest attainable standard of health[170] and education.[171] These rights could be used as the standard for inclusion in the Constitution, thus providing a mechanism for the courts to drive a rights-based approach to social policy without necessarily dictating specific measures.

The argument made against introducing economic and social rights into the Constitution is generally defined by the issue of money. These rights – we are told – produce burdensome responsibilities upon the State because of the perceived cost. The argument is usually attached to the false image of a 'four-bed semi-d with a car outside' for every citizen in the State. But our civil and political rights also have a cost, which often goes unquestioned. The cost of elections; funding political parties; running our judiciary and an Garda Síochána are all costs borne as a result of our civil and political rights. No one argues that the right to be free from crime means we each have to be provided with twenty-four hour police protection.

The argument against socio-economic rights is ultimately a refusal to force the State to deal with its most vulnerable citizens. It is a class and gender argument that places a value on a liberal philosophy of rights, but not a communalist philosophy of rights. Of course there are no circumstances where the State can afford to give excessive provisions to each citizen. However, a model of 'progressive realisation' of rights clearly enumerated in the Constitution can provide an important role for the courts in deciding whether or not the rights of vulnerable or marginalised women are being vindicated to the full extent possible.

Promoting Women's Participation in Politics

At the heart of a new Constitution must be the right of women to participate fully and freely in public affairs. The impact of women's exclusion from Irish public life is felt at every turn in Irish society. Perhaps it is no more visible than in the shocking delays in implementing the provisions of the 'X case' and the two related referenda.

Ireland's lack of progress is very marked in the international context. The Inter-Parliamentary Union (IPU) statistics reveal that Ireland is currently in 88th place globally in representation of women in politics.[172] This is a large drop from our previous position at 37th in 1990. Ireland now lags behind European counterparts who have adopted affirmative action measures to remedy the problem. Representation of women in Dáil Eireann is now at 15.8% with 26 women representatives out of 166.

The status of women in other areas of decision making is similar, if not worse. Our all-powerful sixteen-member Cabinet has two women and fourteen men. Ballot papers are simply lists of men: eight out of ten candidates at the last election. Boardrooms are almost women-free zones; nine out of ten ISEQ board members are men. Eight out of ten senior judges are men. Research by NWCI indicates that only three out of ten voices in current affairs radio belong to women.

There are no perfect systems, but there are models that come close to achieving balance. Democracy often requires 'fine-tuning': it is constantly evolving. Some aspects of democracy, such as free elections, are entirely necessary for a political system to qualify as democratic. However, these aspects alone are not sufficient to constitute a fully representative, complete democratic system. Each country has different needs and priorities and can adapt their system in the ways that work for them in order to enhance democratic legitimacy. In the EU there is great diversity in the types of electoral systems used to select representatives. All of these are perceived as democratic, but it may be that some are more effective than others for ensuring that the voices of both women and men have a chance to be heard.

A new Constitution that was founded on the principle of women's freedom to participate fully in public affairs would seek to address three core areas:

- A symbolic statement of values that recognises civil society groups and encourages active citizenship;
- Strengthening our direct democracy provisions; and
- An electoral system that can create fairer outcomes for women and men seeking political office.

While these provisions are not comprehensive, addressing them would rebalance many of the deficits of the system currently in place. It would place inclusivity and participation at the forefront of our democracy.

Encouraging Active Citizenship and Recognising Civil Society

If the first job of a Constitution is to create a moral and legal framework for a State, then surely the next job must be to create a platform for citizens to engage with it. A Constitution lacking the involvement of its citizens is a body without breath.

Allowing citizens to breathe life into the Constitution is done by acknowledging their value and their role. As individuals, or collectively organised in groups, citizens ought to play a role in shaping the society to which they belong.

Engaging women as full citizens must begin at this symbolic level with an invitation to participate and an acknowledgement that such participation, in whatever form it takes, will produce a benefit to the life of the State. Brady suggests a text along these lines as an appropriate one:[173]

> All citizens, both as individuals and in associations of individual citizens, shall have the opportunity to participate fully and actively in the public life of the State, with a view to enhancing the democratic process, and such participation shall be supported by the State.

Introducing a Direct Democracy Provision

The US political scientist Sherry Arnstein speaks of a 'ladder of citizen participation.'[174] At the top rung of the ladder is citizen control, exercised through delegated power and in a meaningful partnership between the citizen and the organs of the State. On the bottom rung of the ladder is the kind of society we see reflected in Bahrain or Syria, where citizens are subject to manipulation and the control of autocratic governments. In the middle sits today's Ireland: a society where political participation borders on the tokenistic and is characterised by the desire of the political class to placate the citizenry through consultation and the provision of information.

A society based on the principle of meaningful participation is not beyond our capacity – indeed, Bunreacht na hÉireann gives the citizens the final say over changes to the Constitution in a form of citizen participation, the referendum.

The courts observed, in *Hanafin v Minister for the Environment*, that: 'The will of the people as expressed in a referendum providing for the amendment of the Constitution is sacrosanct and if freely given cannot be interfered with. The decision is theirs and theirs alone.'[175]

Referenda are necessarily a blunt tool and, as can be seen in Switzerland, do not always produce progressive measures. However, they fit snugly into the tradition of Irish political and cultural life. As such we should seek a model that is coherent with our existing understanding, but also enhances the power given to people. One model for doing so would be to reapply the version enshrined in the 1922 Constitution, which provided for the people to vote on legislation as well as to initiate referenda. The 1922 mechanism could force politicians to develop a more effective and more participatory system of promulgating laws in order to avoid the embarrassment of having their legislation rejected in a plebiscite.

A Balanced Electoral System

The Irish PR-STV system is one of the great features of our political system. It lends itself to count-night dramatics like few others. The system has also been embraced by the electorate in two separate referenda. Even in recent studies, made at a time when distaste for the political system is particularly evident, the electorate's attachment to the PR-STV system more or less remains.[176]

It is important to note that there is no perfect electoral system for improving the position of women in our democracy. Each system carries with it limitations. What we seek is a system that promotes and reflects the values of the society we wish to live in. A proportional system tends to lead to more diversity in politics than majoritarian systems. However, addressing the problem of the electoral system could help limit some of the problems of Irish politics that prevent women's participation, such as intra-party fighting and parochialism. However, it won't eliminate them, and it is not by itself a panacea to the burning issue of low participation of women in political life or building a more equal society.[177]

There are also opportunities – by reforming the electoral system we can create more mature ways for politics to be conducted, by changing the cultural practices which result from our existing system.

A system used widely across Continental Europe is the proportional representation list system. As Brady writes: 'A list system uses national or large multi-seat regional constituencies in which voters cast their vote for the party of their choice. The seats in the legislature are then divided among the parties according to their share of the vote. In a closed list system, the political parties decide the priority of their candidates for the seats the party wins. In an open list system, the voter is able to express a preference among the party's candidates.'[178]

A wealth of international research indicates that such systems correlate well with a higher proportionate of women elected.[179] For Irish people to jump straight into a provincial or national list system may be simply unpalatable. The electorate would be correctly wary of a system that increases the control of political parties and eliminates all links to constituencies. A balanced approach could be found with a mixed national list and multi-seat constituency system. Although this would not eliminate intra-party factionalism it can provide an alternative career path for politicians who wish to pursue a 'national' career.

In New Zealand, the face of politics was transformed in a short period. The country – similar in size and make-up to our own – opted for a mixed-member proportional system. Previously New Zealand had very low female participation in Parliament (despite the fact that New Zealand was the first country in the world to grant women's suffrage). The changed system is credited with increasing the representation of women to around 30% and by 2002 women won more of the constituency seats than the party list seats.[180] The comparison has its limitations (the NZ system maintained single-seat constituencies), but it suggests that a newly developed system could improve gender equality in the Dáil.

Even maintaining the popular PR-STV system need not be the end of electoral reform. Increasing the size of constituencies will help to ensure that more women are elected. But this should be coupled with a maintenance of the number of Dáil members to ensure that workloads do not become completely unmanageable, particularly as the evidence suggests that women politicians receive more constituency requests than their male counterparts.

Respecting Women's Choices and Diversity

It is in the sphere of culture that some of the most difficult battles for women's equality have been fought. At the core of these battles is a choice between an Ireland that recognises and respects diversity or an Ireland that harks back to an older time when notions of mutual respect were publicly espoused but not always privately lived. As Bacik argues: 'Twenty years ago, Ireland was an infinitely more miserable place: insular, narrow-minded, with little tolerance of diversity ... We were not better people, just poorer.'[181]

In today's Ireland the debate focuses on two areas. Firstly, there is the right of women to make decisions about their own bodies. Secondly, the right of the lesbian and gay population to have their love recognised by the State.

Freedom to Make Decisions About One's Own Body

The freedom to control one's own body is at the heart of what women's equality is about. The lack of access to reproductive health care, including abortion, intersects with other forms of discrimination against women. Any discussion on abortion needs to be discussed within the framework of creating an equal society. Access to safe and legal abortion is indistinguishably linked to human rights values that protect a woman's right to privacy, her right to bodily integrity, her right to self-determination, her right to be free from inhuman, cruel and degrading treatment and her right to accessible, appropriate and quality health care. Failure to provide for safe and legal abortion in Ireland consistently contravenes these rights.

The current Irish constitutional position is extremely unusual compared to that of other States. [182] Our laws are rooted in the Victorian-era Offences Against the Persons Act (1861). The Act criminalises women who 'procure a miscarriage' and those who assist them, e.g., a doctor. It imposes a maximum penalty of life imprisonment in both cases.[183] Abortion in Ireland is an offence in the criminal code, including when there is a threat to the health of the mother, where the pregnancy occurs as a result of rape or incest and also when it has been established that the pregnancy is unviable. However, two referenda as a result of the 'X case'[184] have actually indicated that the citizens of Ireland do not agree with this legislation and want a constitutional right to abortion in situations where there is a threat to the life (including suicide) as opposed to the health of the mother. In a recent opinion poll 85% of respondents supported legislation for the X case; 82% of respondents supported a constitutional amendment to extend the right to abortion to all cases where the health of the mother is seriously threatened and also in cases of rape; and 36% of respondents supported a constitutional amendment to allow for legal abortion in any case where a woman requests it.[185]

The reality is that women in Ireland experience crisis pregnancies[186] and, despite the lack of lawful services in Ireland, the country has an abortion rate. In 2010, according to the Irish Contraception and Crisis Pregnancy Study, one in every seven pregnancies for women in Ireland was a crisis pregnancy,[187] and 21% of crisis pregnancies and 4% of all pregnancies end in abortion.

Women and girls wishing to avail of abortion services must travel outside of Ireland. Figures from the Department of Health in the UK show that in 2011, 4,200 women gave Irish addresses at UK abortion clinics.[188] Many others do not give addresses or travel to countries such as the Netherlands or Spain.[189] In the ten years between 2001 and 2011, 58,618 Irish women and girls obtained an abortion in a clinic in the UK or Wales. An additional 1,470 women obtained an abortion in the Netherlands between 2005 and 2010. Between 1980 and 2011, (http://www.crisispregnancy.ie/news/number-of-women-giving-irish-addresses-at-uk-abortion-clinics-decreases-for-tenth-year-in-a-row-according-to-department-of-health-uk/), at least 152,061 (http://www.ifpa.ie/node/501) women living in Ireland travelled to England and Wales to access safe abortion services. It is important to acknowledge that these figures probably represent an underestimation of the true numbers, as many Irish women do not give an Irish address for reasons of confidentiality.[190] This imposes significant financial, psychological and physical hardship on women, particularly those who have health problems including mental health problems, financial worries, concern about the well-being of other children, or relationship issues. The stress involved in making the decision is exacerbated by having to travel to another country to access abortion services, by the expense involved, by feelings of fear and stigma, by secrecy, by a sense of isolation or by lack of support. The denial of abortion services further disadvantages vulnerable, marginalised and deprived women and girls who cannot raise the necessary funds to travel abroad, who cannot leave the jurisdiction because of immigration restrictions, or who are in the care of the State.

Our new Constitution must incorporate full access to safe and legal abortion in Ireland for women who chose this as the best option for themselves. Even with legislation to give effect to the constitutional right to abortion where there is a real and substantial risk to the life of the mother, Ireland will have one of the most restrictive regimes in the world. Outlawing the procedure does little to deter women seeking abortions.[191] Two options, then, arise in formulating a new constitution.

The first is to remove all reference to the right to life of the unborn from the text. If this were done, then the text of the Constitution would essentially say nothing about abortion. However, as we have seen in Ireland, the courts may still interpret the Constitution to say things about abortion at a later stage. Brady argues that 'pursuit of this option carries very heavy risks of unintended consequences arising from judicial interpretation. The courts could feasibly determine that the right to life in Article 40.3.2 extends to the unborn, which would – effectively – return matters to the current situation.'[192]

The alternative option is to insert a proviso allowing for abortion for health, well-being or other reasons. A proposed text would state that the subsection does not limit the provision of medical termination to terminate pregnancy for certain specified reasons; most obviously the health or well-being of the mother, but a more nuanced basis for permitting termination could also be included. Such a proviso should also very clearly state that such medical terminations must be regulated by law in order to come within the exception to the right to life of the unborn. Such a wordy piece of text also risks judicial interpretation, which is why clear leadership from our legislators to give women the freedom to make informed and empowered decisions about their own bodies could guide the courts in their decision.

The welcome passage of legislation to give effect to the 'X case' should not be seen as the end of the work to ensure women have control over their bodies. This fundamental right needs to be recognised and enjoyed in our new feminist constitution.

The Right to Have Your Love Recognised by the State

The restrictive model of the family in the 1937 Constitution allowed only for a particular, Roman Catholic, understanding of what a family can be. While it may well have reflected the social mores of its time, it remains truly problematic for thousands of lesbian and gay couples throughout Ireland. The impact has been to codify direct discrimination against the choices made by citizens to love freely and to have that love recognised and valued by the State.

This policy has been confirmed by the legislature through the Civil Partnership Act, which included no less than 160 pieces of direct discrimination between lesbian couples and heterosexual couples.[193] It has also been confirmed by the courts in the case of *Zappone and Gilligan v Revenue Commissioners*,[194] where the judgment indicated that Ireland's policy had always been to understand the idea of marriage as between a man and a woman.

The hardship caused to couples denied the right to love freely manifests itself in a range of areas, all now codified in the Civil Partnership Act. This includes providing only for lesbian couples to have ownership of a shared home rather than a family home; denying custody and guardianship to lesbian couples with children; placing the fate of lesbian and gay immigrants with Irish partners into the hands of 'ministerial discretion', and failing to provide full tax equality to people in gay relationships.

Seeking to make our understanding of marriage more compassionate, one model to look at is the Canadian one. A 2004 decision by the Canadian Supreme Court deemed as constitutional an Act permitting full civil marriage equality among same-sex couples.[195] The Canadian court took the view that it was legitimate to interpret the Charter of Rights and Freedoms (which is a bill of rights annexed to the Canadian Constitution) in a contemporary fashion. Their approach also nullified the need for complex marriage equality legislation by simply extending the previous civil marriage provisions to same-sex couples.

Drawing on an existing common-law definition used by the courts in some instances of marriage as a 'solemn contract of partnership,'[196] Brady argues that 'By relying on language that has already been used by the courts, it is feasible to construct a wording which fits in with the existing law on civil marriage … as follows: The civil institution of Marriage as regulated by law is the voluntary union of two persons, based on a solemn contract of partnership and to the exclusion of all others.'

This would have the benefit of updating existing legal practice as well as avoiding any unforeseen – and undesirable – misinterpretations by the courts.

Conclusion

The starting point for our new feminist Constitution must be to create an enabling environment for women to be free and equal. It must be built on the participation of women, valuing the many roles they play in society and seeking to encourage and develop them. By combining a vision of equality with accountability mechanisms that allow individuals to protect their rights we can, finally, begin to overhaul our society.

A New Democratic Programme

Niamh Puirséil

When the first meeting of Dáil Éireann took place on 21 January 1919, it had before it three items of business: a declaration of independence, a message to the free nations of the world calling for recognition of Ireland's independence and, finally, the adoption of the Democratic Programme. In fewer than 600 words in the English language version, the Programme laid out the principles on which the Irish Republic was to be built – those of liberty, equality and justice for all – where every man and woman would give their allegiance to 'the commonwealth' and, in return, each citizen would receive an adequate share of the product of the nation's labour and where the government's first duty would be to ensure the physical, mental and spiritual well-being of every child. The Programme was not framed as a Constitution as such, but it did outline the basic ethos and civic framework on which the new State would be built. Significantly, however, the word 'State' is entirely absent from the text. In contrast, the 1922 Free State Constitution and its 1937 successor, Bunreacht na hÉireann, both focused on drawing up the State's legal and political infrastructure, but the notion of citizenship, and the rights and responsibilities it conferred, was wholly absent, an absence that has been reflected in the political culture of the State. In recent years, particularly in the context of the post-2008 economic crisis and the political re-evaluation which followed (such as it was), this absence of a popular civic republicanism has been highlighted as a factor contributing to Ireland's national malaise by various commentators. This view has much to recommend it, although there is rarely (if ever) any acknowledgement of the voices that had called for the State to promote an active citizenship in the past, but who were readily ignored by those who held political power almost from the outset. The Democratic Programme adopted by Dáil Éireann in January 1919 is probably the most pertinent example, a document that not only remains relevant today, but which is significantly more progressive than anything that followed in the century since it was put before Ireland's first independent Parliament.

Background to the Democratic Programme

To understand the Democratic Programme properly, it is important to consider the immediate context from which it emerged. The first Dáil took place five weeks after the 1918 General Election, which had seen Sinn Féin win an electoral landslide, wiping out the Home Rule Party and ending the monopoly it had held on Irish politics over the previous fifty years.[197] Famously, the Labour Party had not contested the election. Ultimately, after several months of wrangling (external and internal), it had agreed to step down and leave Sinn Féin to a straight fight against the Home Rule candidates, in effect turning the election into a plebiscite on the constitutional issue.[198] This was a considerable sacrifice for Labour, a sacrifice that some analysts argue caused irreparable damage to the party.[199] Others, myself included, disagree, but since the party had been so obliging, Sinn Féin felt inclined to give something back in return. Added to this, however, was the imminent journey by a Labour delegation to the Socialist International in Berne, which was beginning on 3 February. In Berne, the two Irish Labour men (Tom Johnson, treasurer of the Irish Labour Party and Trade Union Congress, and Cathal O'Shannon, an official in the Irish Transport and General Workers Union) would lobby for support for Irish self-determination, and it seemed that anything that might lend progressive or radical credentials to the new government would surely 'strengthen the delegation's hand in Switzerland.'[200]

If the desire to keep Labour onside, repay it for 1918 and to court favour with the socialists in Berne were the main factors in asking Johnson and his colleagues to write the Dáil's social programme, there was another consideration: there were few others capable of doing the job. Sinn Féin itself had little or nothing in the way of a social or economic policy; as Fr O'Flanagan was said to have observed after the 1918 Election, 'the people have voted Sinn Féin. What we have to do now is to explain to them what Sinn Féin is.'[201] Part of the problem was that 'Sinn Féin', that broad alliance of disparate political beliefs, had not given the issue a great deal of thought. Many of those who had been inclined towards political thinking had died in 1916 and their successors seemed, for the most part, of a less philosophical bent. Theirs was an attitude summed up in a story told by Seán O'Faolain, about an English journalist who visited Dublin after 1916. He plied the general secretary of Sinn Féin, Paudeen O'Keeffe, 'with so many insistent questions on the lines of "What are the practical aims of this movement?" and got so many unsatisfactory answers that, in the end, he said in some slight exasperation: "Mr O'Keeffe, would you at least say what exactly you yourself want?" At this O'Keeffe banged his desk and roared: "Vingeance, bejasus!"'[202]

Similarly, in his history of Sinn Féin between 1916 and 1923, Michael Laffan has observed that Sinn Féin 'did not engage in the sort of intellectual debates which pre-occupied many of their counterparts in other countries.'[203] It would be wrong to suggest that these debates did not take place at all, but within Sinn Féin people who thought in a practical way about the nature of Irish society after the revolution, people such as Liam Mellows, were in the minority and tended to be on the left. For the rest, Connolly's idea of 'painting the postboxes green' did not seem too objectionable at all. As such, another factor in Johnson being asked to write the programme was because he could, and there was no one in Sinn Féin who would be equal to the job.

Its precise genesis is somewhat unclear, but it seems that Sinn Féin, in the person of Seán T. O'Kelly, approached Labour to write a social and economic programme for the new Dáil, and that talks between the two parties on the subject began in early January 1919. In the middle of the month, the Labour contingent met with Sinn Féin representatives and presented them with the document they planned to present in Berne. Afterwards, Sinn Féin released a statement noting that they 'heartily approved' of the document and that a committee had been 'appointed to draw up the draft of a programme of constructive work on democratic lines in consultation with the Labour leaders.'[204] In reality, however, there was no committee, and the task of writing the programme was left largely in the hands of Tom Johnson, with input from his colleagues Cathal O'Shannon and William O'Brien (the ITGWU's acting general secretary).[205]

Years later, Cathal O'Shannon observed that their draft programme was not a Labour Party production and would have 'probably been worded differently' if that had been the case,[206] but instead (at O'Shannon's suggestion[207]) Johnson began his draft by quoting from the 1916 Proclamation, and then from Patrick Pearse's last major pamphlet (published on 31 March 1916), *The Sovereign People*. This was in order to 'link Easter Week with the Dáil's need for a social policy' as well as to illustrate the influence that James Connolly had had on Pearse's thought in later years.[208] In Pearse's words, the passage asserted that 'no private right to property is good against the public right of the Nation … whenever forms of productive wealth are wrongfully used … the Nation shall resume possession without compensation.' The draft continued in a similar vein, asserting that 'the Irish Republic shall always count wealth and prosperity by the measure of health and happiness of its citizens' and, as such, the first duty of the government of the Republic would be to make provision for the physical, mental and spiritual well-being of the children. It set out how natural resources would be exploited for the good of the people and how where 'productive wealth' was 'wrongfully used or withheld from use to the detriment of the Republic, there the nation shall resume possession without compensation.'

Having dealt with trade, and noting that 'it shall be the purpose of the government to encourage the organisation of the people into trade unions and co-operative societies with a view to the control and administration of the industries by the workers engaged in the industries.' Finally, it concluded that 'the Republic will aim at the elimination of the class in society which lives upon the wealth produced by the workers of the nation but gives no useful service in return, and in the process of accomplishment will bring freedom to all who have hitherto been caught in the toils of economic servitude.'[209]

Johnson's document, however, was far from the last word since, as Aindrias Ó Cathasaigh has noted, 'the republicans were not minded to let the programme through on the nod.'[210] Michael Collins called a meeting of leading members of the IRB for the eve of the inaugural session of the first Dáil to consider the Democratic Programme. According to P. S. O'Hegarty, one of those present: 'The Democratic Programme gave rise to a lively debate, the preponderance of opinion being against it. It was urged that this declaration was in fact ultra vires for the Dáil, whose one and only business was to get the English out of Ireland, and that all internal and arguable questions like this should be left over until the English had actually been got out, and, on a vote, that view was upheld. Collins then said that he would suppress the Democratic Programme, and he did so; but, next morning, the others refused to go on without a Democratic Programme, and the draft was handed to Seán T. O'Kelly, who finally produced what was put before the Dáil.'[211]

O'Kelly's recollection differed somewhat, but as Ó Cathasaigh observes, 'his description of how the draft was received rings true: '[There was] a long and sometimes heated discussion. There were ideas and statements which some of the committee would not accept. The discussion lasted until well after eleven o'clock ... Eventually the meeting broke up without any agreement. All notes and suggestions were thrown at me because I was chairman. I was told to draft the document myself.'[212]

As Ó Cathasaigh observes, 'O'Shannon thought that the Sinn Féin executive, with O'Kelly's own support, overruled the IRB objections,'[213] and O'Kelly was given the task of rendering Johnson's original document into something that the IRB would find less objectionable. O'Kelly worked through the night, cutting extensively, editing other sections but adding little of his own. He removed some of the more radical elements in the text, including the elimination of the capitalist class and the confiscation of misused property, and rephrased other sections. Years later, O'Shannon compared the original draft and the final version and found that around half of the Johnson draft was omitted.[214] Once O'Kelly had finished his revisions, there was a rush to have the final version typed up for the opening of the Dáil. With no time left to write an Irish translation, Piaras Béaslaí was left to do an impromptu translation, pretending to read from the English text.[215] As O'Kelly later recalled, 'the draft of the Democratic Programme was not submitted to any committee or indeed to any individual except my wife,'[216] and Cathal O'Shannon noted that it was not until he and Johnson listened to the programme being read to the Dáil that they realised that it had been amended. Indeed, it was only years later that they discovered what had happened. But while much of the explicit socialism of the first draft was excised, it was not wholly eliminated, and the end result did not trouble Johnson (or O'Shannon) a great deal, if at all. Johnson had wept with emotion as it was read out, and O'Shannon recalled that he had had to prevent him from disturbing the solemn proceedings by cheering.[217]

Although it is a short document, I will just quote a couple of excerpts here:

'We declare that the Nation's sovereignty extends not only to all men and women of the Nation, but to all its material possessions, the Nation's soil and all its resources, all the wealth and all the wealth-producing processes within the Nation, and ... we reaffirm that all right to private property must be subordinated to the public right and welfare.

We declare that we desire our country to be ruled in accordance with the principles of Liberty, Equality, and Justice for all, which alone can secure permanence of Government in the willing adhesion of the people.

We affirm the duty of every man and woman to give allegiance and service to the Commonwealth, and declare it is the duty of the Nation to assure that every citizen shall have opportunity to spend his or her strength and faculties in the service of the people. In return for willing service, we, in the name of the Republic, declare the right of every citizen to an adequate share of the produce of the Nation's labour.

It shall be the first duty of the Government of the Republic to make provision for the physical, mental and spiritual well-being of the children, to secure that no child shall suffer hunger or cold from lack of food, clothing, or shelter, but that all shall be provided with the means and facilities requisite for their proper education and training as Citizens of a Free and Gaelic Ireland.'

Johnson's enthusiasm was quite understandable; the meeting itself was a momentous occasion in its own right but to see it adopt a radical social and economic programme, based on his words, was remarkable. The question of whether anyone in Sinn Féin took the programme seriously had been debated for decades. Some have argued that it was genuine, others that it was a mere sop to Labour, but considering how the programme was ignored subsequently, Johnson's enthusiasm was misplaced.

The IRB was opposed, as we have noted already, not merely to its content but to its being read at all. In later years, there were others on the Cumann na nGaedheal/ Fine Gael side who were openly contemptuous of it. Asked about the programme fifty years later, in 1969, Ernest Blythe recalled, 'no, I never found anybody who took the slightest interest in it. The Labour Party secured the adoption of it. I don't think anybody, practically speaking, bothered with it afterwards. It was regarded as some sort of hoisting of a flag. It wasn't regarded as significant in the struggle that was commencing.'[218] Similarly, Piaras Béaslaí, who was on the Dáil preparatory committee (and who 'read' the Irish version to the assembly) later wrote that it was doubtful whether a majority of the members would have voted for it, without amendment, had there been any immediate prospect of putting it into force.' If Béaslaí has been accused of taking a reactionary view of the document in retrospect, it certainly did not take long before it had taken on the appearance of a dead letter.[219] The first instance was in a speech by Éamon de Valera, President of the Republic, in April 1919. De Valera had played no part in the drafting or adoption of the programme as he had been in Lincoln Jail at the time. Speaking only a couple of months afterwards, he told deputies that the Democratic Programme contemplated a situation somewhat different from that in which they actually found themselves. He had never made any promise to Labour, because, 'while the enemy was within their gates, the immediate question was to get possession of their country.'[220]

By 1922, the British enemy had moved beyond the gates. The Anglo–Irish treaty meant that there was now a new Free State government facing a new republican adversary. On the anti-treaty side of Sinn Féin, there was little attention given to social policy as they focused wholly on fighting the civil war. The exception was Liam Mellows, whose *Notes from Mountjoy Jail* (published on 21 September 1922) called for the Democratic Programme to be 'translated into something definite', but his more militarily minded superiors in the IRA disagreed, with Liam Lynch, echoing de Valera three years earlier, arguing that the time 'had not yet arrived' for adopting 'a republican democratic programme.[221]

At the same time, the Cumann na nGaedheal government was drafting a Free State Constitution. The Anglo–Irish treaty put significant limits on some of its political provisions, but on other issues it had full room to manoeuvre. It became abundantly clear, however, that the concepts of prescriptive rights and belief in the community which had shaped the Democratic Programme were regarded as anathema to the Cumann na nGaedheal government.[222] It was a middle-class, deeply Catholic administration, which wholly refused to consider the idea of a Constitution that guaranteed rights or did anything to introduce 'big government.' This was perhaps most obvious in its ministers' response to an amendment on education tabled by the Labour deputy, T. J. O'Connell. Drawing heavily from the Democratic Programme, it began: 'the right of the child to food, clothing, shelter and education, sufficient for their proper physical welfare and training as citizens of Saorstát Éireann is guaranteed,' and concluded: 'All schools and educational establishments shall aim at inculcating moral character, religious tolerance, and personal and vocational efficiency, and that the teaching given therein shall be imbued with the spirit of Irish nationality and international goodwill. The duties of citizenship shall be a subject of instruction in all schools in order to fit the pupil for his responsibilities as a citizen.'[223]

Kevin O'Higgins responded that constitutions should only include 'fundamental rights' and that all that was needed was 'the minimum', while his colleague Ernest Blythe opined, 'I think it would be pretty well agreed that the Amendment as drafted would not be a proper one to put into the Constitution.' Cathal O'Shannon, who had contributed to the Democratic Programme, countered, 'here in the document that is to be the framework of the whole future legislation of the country, the very people who are to be the citizens of the future State – the children who are the foundation of the State and the foundation of the family – the position of the children, of the family, of the education, and every provision for the children is to be neglected in the fundamental legislation of the country.[224] But the idea of citizenship was nowhere to be seen in the Free State Constitution. The Treaty may have curtailed the new Constitution in some key aspects (most obviously in the position of the monarch and the oath), but it was not the Treaty that prevented the drafters of the Free State Constitution from identifying the new State as a republic in all but name, one where (in the words of the Democratic Programme) 'the duty of every man and woman [is] to give allegiance and service to the commonwealth'. That the word 'commonwealth' did not appear at all is not surprising. The term had been interchangeable with 'republic' in England for centuries, most notably during the seventeenth century, where its was used by political philosophers, most notably Thomas Hobbes and John Locke, and lent its name to the Cromwellian regime (1649–60). It was fashionable among writers on the left in the late nineteenth and early twentieth century, spanning French syndicalists and British social democrats whose stated goal was to establish the 'co-operative commonwealth.'[225] The Cromwellian connotations did little to make the word popular. During the Dublin Lockout of 1913, William Martin Murphy deliberately invoked its other meaning when he claimed that Jim Larkin sought the establishement of a co-operative commonwealth 'in which he, no doubt, was to be Cromwell.'[226] By 1922, however, it was more immediately associated with the British Empire, which had recently redefined itself as the 'British Commonwealth of Nations' (as enshrined in Article 1 of the Free State

Constitution). But what was in a name? What it boiled down to was not that the government disliked the word 'commonwealth' for any reason, it was that its members had no affinity with what it stood for. Whether it was 'commonwealth', 'republic' or even 'nation', it was the individual, not the collective, which was at the heart of the new State's philosophy as outlined in its first Constitution. Michael Laffan has noted of Sinn Féin (1916–23) that 'they preached the merits of a republic but did not discuss such "republican" concepts as the rights and duties of the citizen,'[227] which is true, up to a point, but here we can see how when Labour tried to raise these questions they were abruptly dismissed. It was not that these issues were not considered, it was that the idea of a republic of equals who, through their fulfilment of the duties of citizenship, then had entitlements from the State, was intolerable to the people in government whose attitude towards how the new State should look were defined by their religion and class, representing 'the best elements of society' as they saw themselves.[228]

Later, when the debate moved to natural resources, Kevin O'Higgins made his views abundantly clear, accusing Labour of trying to embody communist doctrine into the Free State Constitution. Johnson countered that it was in the Democratic Programme. 'That is not a Constitution' was O'Higgins response. Johnson's response to O'Higgins is perhaps as valid now as it was then: 'It is quite evident from the last two speeches that there is a very different conception of the purpose of a Constitution in the minds of ministers and in the minds of those of us who are sitting here,' he said. 'As a matter of practice, as a matter of precedent, we find that constitutions are usually made at a time when the public mind is flexible and after a leap forward, and it is with the desire that the opinions of the best minds of the best period shall be fixed that Constitutions are made. It is quite evident in the minds of Ministers and their supporters that we should be as limited, as conservative as possible, and do nothing that would suggest that there has been a revolution, but rather to accept the position which we have arrived at through English legislation with just some little change in the political arrangement of the country and stand at that and not move forward … I think it is a pity that we are not intending to embody in the Constitution the best thoughts of the best period in Irish history.'[229]

Clearly, however, this was not to be, and when Éamon de Valera came to draft a new Constitution more than a decade later, he was no more inclined to be radical. It was less minimal than its predecessor, but where it was prescriptive, it was not necessarily progressive, most obviously in the sections in Article 41 relating to the role of women.

Bunreacht na hÉireann retained one of the key problems with the Free State Constitution, namely, that no real relationship was set out between the State and its citizens. There was an Irish nation that affirmed its 'inalienable, indefeasible and sovereign right' to self-determination, and there was a State whose apparatus was set out in the Constitution, but the notion of a commonwealth of which all were part, or the concept of citizenship in a republic (which dared not speak its name), was entirely absent.

Perhaps, one could argue, this was because now, almost twenty years after it had been adopted, the Democratic Programme was a dead letter, long forgotten, but that was not the case. For many years, the Corú (constitution) of Fianna Fáil listed one of the party's seven aims as being 'to carry out the Democratic Programme of the First Dáil', but when the opportunity presented itself to enshrine part or all of the programme in the State's Constitution, de Valera ignored its existence entirely. Its civic republicanism did not fit with de Valera's desire to build his basic law on Catholic social teaching and the idea of subsidiarity, which was arguably implicit in the minimalism of the 1922 Constitution. This is summed up in Article 41.1.1, which asserts: 'The State recognises the family as the natural primary and fundamental unit group of society.' In other words, the State is built not on a collective or 'commonwealth' of citizens but is a collection of families. The suspicion of the State was not merely the result of Catholic social teaching's emphasis on the family and fear of secular government. The manner in which this State came into being led to many people holding an ambiguous view of it, which reinforced the lack of engagement with the idea of the State. The Seán Citizen of the *Dublin Opinion* cartoons was not an active participant in his State but an unfortunate soul who suffered under its vagaries.

Although in practice there was little evidence of its influence, the fulfilment of the Democratic Programme remained a stated aim of two of the three main parties in the State, i.e., Fianna Fáil and Labour, even though in Fianna Fáil's case, it tended to emphasise its first two aims (reunification and the revival of the Irish language) to the exclusion of all others. Still, while the programme was never entirely forgotten, it enjoyed something of a revival in the mid to late 1960s, when its radicalism chimed with the spirit of social and political rebellion, and the fiftieth anniversary of the Easter Rising encouraged a return to the foundations of the modern State. Writing in 1969, the economist Patrick Lynch, then lecturing in UCD, noted the changes in attitude which had begun in recent years 'when young people saw that there are individuals in all three political parties who appear to have more in common with themselves and with the Democratic Programme … than with the policies of our political parties at the last general election.'[230]

Not that its appeal was limited to the new generation. Seán Lemass referred to it in several speeches during his time as Taoiseach and, privately at least, he had expressed a desire to restate its social objectives. The observations of Michael McInerney, political correspondent of *The Irish Times* in 1964, are worth quoting at length: 'Our Constitution is now almost 30 years old and was written also when political aims were predominant. Its social provisions are not very comprehensive but one serious theory put forward by one who was involved is that it envisaged that the Dáil would later formulate a social charter without challenge by the Constitution. But the State exists without any formal comprehensive declaration of social principles, apart from what is explicit in government practice and legislation. The policy that "social aims must wait" had become a habit. It is possible that consequently we are all still very much influenced by the liberal ethic that "all's fair in love, war, and also in business and politics." At the same time the Taoiseach is trying to bid "au revoir to laissez-faire" and to turn the nation's mind towards a community outlook, towards a new code of social morals. This policy of the new role of government really is one of the great phenomena of the Ireland of today. The government and State are accepted as the organiser of social equality and of economic growth. This new concept that the State and government represent the people and are no longer the enemy is another factor inspiring the call for a social charter. If the government is going to have so much power then the people must know how it is going to be used.'[231]

McInerney, at least, seemed to think that Lemass would use the commemorations of the 1916 rising to 'declare in 1966 terms the national aims as defined in the 1919 programme',[232] and when the Taoiseach established an All-party Committee on the Constitution that year it looked as though this might actually become a reality. Chaired by Deputy George Colley, it issued a report in 1967 and the following year saw a draft report drawn up by the Attorney General, but nothing came of it. One crucial factor was that the unfolding conflict in Northern Ireland overtook thoughts of constitutional change,[233] but perhaps personnel were important too. The Convention was Lemass's baby; Jack Lynch, his successor as Taoiseach, was more socially and politically conservative. In the end, the only recommendation he took up was the removal of PR-STV, which was put before the people in a referendum for the second time in a decade and was roundly defeated. Others were initially ignored (the call to remove the special position of the Catholic Church was shelved until 1972) while there was no desire to remove the constitutional prohibition on divorce.

As it turned out, then, there was no new social charter based on the programme or revision of the Constitution based on its ethos. The report produced by the constitutional review committee may have advised important reforms to Bunreacht na hÉireann, but it bore few hallmarks of the Democratic Programme. The celebrations surrounding 1966 emphasised the Proclamation of the Republic not its successor from the First Dáil and by its anniversary in 1969 it merely highlighted the State's sins of omission. When members of the Oireachtas and distinguished guests met to commemorate the fiftieth anniversary of the First Dáil's inaugural meeting, President de Valera's address was interrupted. 'The programme of the old Dáil has never been implemented. This is a mockery.' The man who interrupted was not some young hothead but Joseph Clarke, who sat in the distinguished visitors' section. Not only was Clarke a veteran of 1916 (he had fought at Mount Street Bridge under de Valera's command), but he had been the usher-in-charge of the first Dáil, which lent some weight to his protest. Later, after Jack Lynch had addressed the gathering, Senator Owen Sheehy Skeffington asked the Taoiseach whether he saw 'the likelihood of the Democratic Programme of the First Dáil being implemented in the foreseeable future, or does he feel that it will continue to remain largely a dead letter?' but he was ruled out of order by the Ceann Comhairle.[234]

Once Lemass had retired from politics, the document's status diminished within Fianna Fáil and became almost exclusively identified with the left, where it continued to be seen as a founding document of a republic that had failed to be. It was spoken of with a certain reverence in the official and provisional wings of the republican movement, and (not surprisingly) was highly regarded in the Labour Party, but otherwise it fell out of favour. It was generally ignored, and where it was not ignored it was derided. Writing in January 1989, Mary Holland noted how 'the political parties achieved a new and rather depressing consensus … when they agreed, unanimously, not to commemorate the seventieth anniversary of the first Dáil.'[235] A suggestion by a Labour senator that the upper house mark the event – highlighting the importance of the Democratic Programme – prompted Senator John A. Murphy to declare it 'a piece of eyewash … mere window dressing.'[236] Senator Murphy's iconoclasm is well known among history students and beyond, but his remarks were part of a long-running narrative that argued that the programme was not representative and was a dead letter from the word go. It was not until the ninetieth anniversary of the First Dáil in 2009, coinciding with the early period of economic crisis, although pre-dating the arrival of the Troika, that attention turned to the programme once again. Among the political parties, Labour (naturally) held a number of events to highlight the programme and its role in its production. Elsewhere, commentators such as Vincent Browne and Fintan O'Toole wrote of its values and its foresight and the extent to which it had been ignored by successive governments. Politically, no one in recent times has identified so strongly with it as President Michael D. Higgins, who probably articulated his point best in his valedictory speech to Dáil Éireann in January 2011. On that occasion he spoke of his belief that 'no real republic has been created in Ireland' and pointed to the lack of citizenship, not only in Ireland but in the European Union as a whole, and emphasised the need to rebuild an entirely different society, one based on 'political participation, administrative fairness and the equality of the right to community', which included 'a floor of citizenship below which people would not be allowed to fall.'[237]

The picture he painted of a 'radical inclusive republic' was compelling, but, as President Higgins might lament, it was not new. The themes he set out in this speech, in effect a reiteration of the Democratic Programme, would be at the heart of his presidential campaign. He returned to them in his address following his inauguration as President of Ireland. President Higgins quoted the *seanfhocal* '*ní neart go cur le chéile*', translating it in terms Tom Johnson would have understood: 'our strength lies in our common weal, our social solidarity.'

If it is the economic and social elements of the Programme that are emphasised, the absence of the practical republic underlies the critique. From a socialist or social justice perspective, there is much to commend the Democratic Programme, but arguably nothing has done more damage to the course of this State than the elision of the notion of citizenship from our constitutions or the institutions under which they operate, which saw the Sinn Féin revolution consolidated into a nation of mé féiners. It is in part the failure to establish a sense of community among the citizens of the State that allows gross economic inequality and an absence of solidarity to flourish. As Fintan O'Toole pointed out:

'Sometimes you forget how tenuous and fragile a thing is the Irish State, how little it means to so many of its citizens. By the State, I don't mean the nation, the flag, pride in being Irish – all that visceral emotion. I mean, rather, two rational things, one tangible, the other abstract. The State is a set of institutions – the Government, the Oireachtas, the Civil Service, public services, the law, the courts. It is also a broad but crucial sense of mutual dependence – the idea that there's a collective self that goes beyond the narrow realms of family and locality.'[238]

The Constitutional Convention established by the Fine Gael–Labour government in 2012 contains nothing to address this fundamental absence of citizenship. It sets out to debate inconsequential minor reforms, such as the reduction of the voting age, and other issues such as equal marriage rights, blasphemy legislation and the role of women in the Constitution, which do not need discussion but simple reform. Why debate the idea that women and men should be equal citizens under the Constitution? Surely this, if nothing else, is self-evident. The equality of citizenship should be obvious, anyway. Meanwhile, other more contentious issues, most notably abortion, were ignored altogether while a proposal to abolish the Seanad was put directly to the electorate without consideration by the convention.

A Constitution full of platitudinous aspirations is worse than nothing. In 1982, the then Senator John A. Murphy described Article 45 of the current Constitution as coming closer to the Democratic Programme than any other Article, but followed this by describing it as 'pious codswallop.'[239] In a cynical country, which may be more cynical than ever (with good reason), there is no room for pious codswallop but there is, I think, a desire to set things straight. There is an opportunity now to return to the idea. There is strong support for the idea that a new Constitution should include a Bill of Rights, and this was backed up by an Amnesty-sponsored Red C poll. It should not surprise us that in the current context when access to health, housing and security are under attack, that these social and economic rights should be wholly off the agenda for the Constitutional Convention at a time when it was never more necessary to debate these fundamental provisions.

It would be naïve to suggest that a Constitution can be a cure-all for Irish society and that by drafting a number of feel-good clauses about citizenship all the nation's ills would end. Clearly not. Constitutions tend to reflect societies, not shape them, and besides, the degree to which their spirit or letter is followed is open to question. Nevertheless, the document on which the State is built ought to provide more than a basic legal framework: it should help guide us as a society, and if it is the case that 'we are where we are', it can help establish a road map for where we would like to go. If, as Tom Johnson argued in 1922, 'Constitutions are usually made at a time when the public mind is flexible and after a leap forward,' we ought to remember the missed opportunities of the past. To find a Constitution for the twenty-first century, it is worth looking back.

Biographical Notes On Contributors

Maura Adshead

Maura Adshead teaches Irish Politics and Public Policy in the Department of Politics and Public Administration at the University of Limerick. Recent books include (with Jonathon Tonge), *Government and Politics in Ireland. Unity and diversity on a two-polity island*, (Palgrave, 2009); and (with Peadar Kirby and Michelle Millar) *Contesting the State: lessons from the Irish case* (Manchester University Press, 2008). She has published a number of book chapters and articles in academic journals on aspects of Irish politics and policy and has carried out commissioned research for Combat Poverty, the HSE and the NESF.

Ivana Bacik

Senator Ivana Bacik is Reid Professor of Criminal Law at Trinity College Dublin, and a practising barrister. She is a Labour Party Senator for Dublin University (elected 2007 and re-elected 2011), and Deputy Leader of Seanad Eireann. Her publications include *Kicking and Screaming: Dragging Ireland into the Twenty-First Century* (O'Brien, 2004).

Eoin Daly

Dr Eoin Daly is a lecturer in the School of Law at University College Dublin, where he teaches Constitutional Law, Legal Theory, and Law and Religion. His research focuses on the relationship between constitutional law and political theory, with a particular focus on constitutional secularism and legal issues surrounding religion in schools. Eoin Daly is author of *Religion, Law and the Irish State: the Constitutional Framework in Context* (Clarus, 2012). He has also recently published papers in *Legal Studies, the European Journal of Political Theory, Jurisprudence* and the *Oxford Journal of Legal Studies.*

Tom Hickey

Dr Tom Hickey is a lecturer at the School of Law and Government at Dublin City University and a Visiting Professor in Law at the Montesquieu University, Bordeaux IV. He was previously a University Fellow at the School of Law, National University of Ireland, Galway. Tom was also a Visiting Research Scholar at the Center for Human Values, Princeton University (Spring 2009) and at the School of Law, University of Glasgow (Summer 2012). He completed an LL.M. at Cambridge University in 2005 and a Ph.D. at NUI Galway in 2010. He teaches various subjects in public law and legal philosophy. His research, which generally draws on republican scholarship, addresses issues in constitutional law and theory.

Eoin Ó Broin

Eoin Ó Broin is a Sinn Féin activist based in Dublin. He is a political and policy advisor to Pearse Doherty TD and a member of the party's Ard Comhairle. He is author of three books: *Matxinada, Basque Nationalism and Radical Basque Youth Movements* (Left republican Books, 2003), *Sinn Féin and the Politics of Left Republicanism* (Pluto Press, 2009), and *A Better Ireland: Arguments for a New Republic* (Pluto Press, 2013). He writes regularly for *An Phoblacht, Irish Left Review* and *Politico*. You can read his blog on www.eoinobroin.ie and follow him on Twitter @EOBroin.

Donncha O'Connell

Professor Donncha O'Connell is a lecturer in Law at NUI Galway, where he teaches Constitutional Law and European Human Rights. He is a part-time commissioner of the Law Reform Commission and a member of the Legal Aid Board. Donncha edits the *Irish Human Rights Law Review,* published biennially by Clarus Press. He was, from 1999 to 2002, the first full-time director of the Irish Council for Civil Liberties and later served a term as Dean of Law at NUI Galway from 2005 to 2008. He was, until 2012, a board member of the London-based NGO, INTERIGHTS. He is a member of the Board of Directors of the internationally acclaimed Druid Theatre Company.

Orla O'Connor

Orla O'Connor is Director of the National Women's Council of Ireland (NWCI), Ireland's leading representative body for women's organisations. Previously she worked as Head of Policy with the NWCI. Her work has included a broad range of representational work, policy development and analysis including leading the negotiations for the

NWCI in two national social partnership agreements, and representing the NWCI on the National Economic and Social Council. Prior to working with the NWCI she led a community-based centre for the unemployed in Finglas, and developed many local projects to combat unemployment, poverty and social exclusion.

Niamh Puirséil

Dr Niamh Puirséil is a historian and writer. She has written widely on Irish politics and the trade union movement, including *The Irish Labour Party 1922-73* (UCD Press, 2007), the standard history of that party. A former research fellow in the Centre for Contemporary Irish History, TCD, she has previously lectured in UCD and is currently writing a history of the Irish National Teachers Organisation.

Notes

1 The *Guardian*, 19 September 2012.

2 *The Irish Times*, 5 January 2013.

3 Inglehart, Ronald (2008) *Changing Values among Western Publics from 1970 to 2006*. West European Politics 31/1–2, pp. 130–46.

4 Runciman, David (7 June 2012) 'Confusion is power' *London Review of Books*, 34/11, pp. 3–5.

5 Christensen, C. (2011) 'Twitter revolutions? Addressing social media and dissent', *Journal of Computer-Mediated Communication,* 13: 210–30; Shirky, C., (2011) 'The political power of social media', *Foreign Affairs,* 90/1: 28–41.

6 Gladwell, Malcolm (2010) 'Small change: why the revolution will not be tweeted', *The New Yorker,* 14 October 2010, available at: http://www.newyorker.com/reporting/2010/10/04/101004fa_fact_gladwell.

7 Morozov, E. (2009) 'The brave new world of slacktivism', *Foreign Policy,* available at: http://neteffect.foreignpolicy.com/posts/2009/05/19/the_brave_new_world_of_slacktivism.

8 Collins, Neil and O'Shea, Mary (2003) 'Clientelism: facilitating rights and favours' in Adshead, M. and Millar, M. (eds.) *Public Administration and Public Policy in Ireland. Theory and Methods,* London: Routledge, pp. 88–107.

9 Gallagher, Michael (2003) 'Stability and turmoil: analysis of the results' in Gallagher, M., Marsh, M. and Mitchell, P. (eds.) *How Ireland Voted 2002*, p. 102.

10 Ibid.

11 RTÉ News, 10 May 2007, 'Election 2007: Health focus in campaign', available at: http://www.rte.ie/news/2007/0510/election.html.

12 RTÉ News, 10 February 2011, 'Surge in number of Independent candidates', available at: http://www.rte.ie/news/2011/0209/politics.html.

13 Farrell, Brian (1985) 'From friends and neighbours to clients and partisans: some dimensions of parliamentary representation under PR-STV' in Bogdanor, V. (ed.) *Representatives of the People? Parliamentarians and constituents in western democracies,* Aldershot: Gower, p. 14.

14 Boland, J. (1991) 'Dáil can only be reformed if TDs are liberated from multi-seat constituencies', *Representation,* 30/111; FitzGerald, G. (1991) 'The Irish electoral system: defects and possible reforms', *Representation,* 30/111: 49–53, FitzGerald, G. (2003) *Reflections on the Irish State,* Dublin: Irish Academic Press; Martin, M. (1991) 'Fianna Fail has a problem – it's time to deal with it', *Sunday Tribune,* 4 August, p.12; Hussey, G. (1993) *Ireland today: anatomy of a changing state,* Dublin: Townsend, Viking; Dempsey, N. (2006) proposals to reduce the number of TDs from 166 to 120 or fewer in Dáil debates, quoted in McDonald 'Clientelist system must be replaced by effective alternative', *The Irish Times,* 21 April 2006.

15 *Sunday Independent*, 8 August 2006.

16 *The Irish Times,* 21 April 2006.

17 *Limerick Leader*, 11 January 2013, 'Minister Michael Noonan officially opens new Eason store in Limerick', available at: http://www.limerickleader.ie/news/business/minister-michael-noonan-officially-opens-new-eason-store-in-limerick-1-4202441.

18 Murphy, Mary (2008) 'Towards a more equitable society: the role of civil society' in Cronin, M. and Kirby, P. (eds.) *Transforming Ireland: challenges, resources, opportunities,* Manchester: Manchester University Press.

19 Bacik, Ivana (2004) *Kicking and Screaming: Dragging Ireland into the 21st Century*, Dublin: O'Brien Press, pp. 106–131.

20 *The Irish Times,* 14 November 2012, 'Woman denied a termination dies in hospital', available at: http://www.irishtimes.com/newspaper/frontpage/2012/1114/1224326575203.html.

21 *The Irish Times,* 11 January 2012, 'Savita Halappanavar' available at: http://www.irishtimes.com/blogs/poplife/2012/11/14/savitahalappanavar/.

22 The *Guardian,* 16 November 2012 'Savita Halappanavar's death has transformed Irish abortion debate. Abortion is now part of Irish life – what is needed is a referendum on giving women easier access', available at: http://www.guardian.co.uk/commentisfree/2012/nov/16/savita-halappanavar-death-irish-abortion-debate; *Kildare Nationalist,* 6 December 2012, 'Fine Gael backbencher demands abortion referendum', available at: http://www.kildare-nationalist.ie/ 2012/12/06/fine-gael-backbencher-demands-abortion-referendum/; Radio Kerry News, 10 January 2013, 'Catholic Church demands referendum to reverse X case judgement', available at: http://www.radiokerry.ie/news/catholic-church-demands-referendum-to-reverse-x-case-judgement/.

23 *Irish Examiner* Opinion Piece (June 7, 2012) 'Referendum result hasn't settled debate on contentious issue' available at: http://www.irishexaminer.com/opinion/kfsngbeygboj/

24 Seanad Éireann Committee on Procedure and Privileges, Sub-Committee on Seanad Reform (2004) *Report on Seanad Reform*, Dublin Stationery Office: Government of Ireland, p. 26.

25 *The Irish Times,* 5 January 1991.
26 Ward, Alan J. (1996) 'The constitution review group and the "executive state" in Ireland', *Administration*, 44/4: 42–63, p. 55.
27 *The Irish Times*, 20 January 1991.
28 Interview A (15/02/06) National Centre for Partnership and Performance.
29 Ibid.
30 Interview B (08/02/06) Irish Business and Employers Federation.
31 Interview A, *op.cit.*
32 Thomas, Damian (2003) 'Social Partnership in Ireland 1987–2000: an evolving economic and social governance', unpublished PhD dissertation, University of Newcastle, Newcastle Upon Tyne, p. 213.
33 O'Donnell, Rory (2008) 'The partnership state: building the ship at sea' in Adshead, M., Kirby, P. and Millar, M. (eds.) *Contesting the State: Lessons from the Irish Case,* Manchester: Manchester University Press, p. 76.
34 Government of Ireland (1994) *Government of Renewal – 1994 Programme for Government*, Dublin: DSO.
35 Interview B, *op.cit;* Interview C (08/02/06). Department of the Taoiseach.
36 Interview C *op.cit.*
37 Interview D (09/02/06) Small Firms Association.
38 Interview F (16/02/06) Irish Cooperative Organisation Society.
39 Adshead, M. and Millar, M. (2008) 'An examination of Social Exclusion policies, procedures and practices in the context of the National Anti-Poverty Strategy', *Research Report for Combat Poverty*, December 2008, p. 13.
40 Spring, D. (1997) What the Politicians Say, *Poverty Today*, Special Issue on NAPs, 36: 11–12.

41 Combat Poverty Agency (2000) *Planning for a More Inclusive Society: An Initial Assessment of the NAPS. Dublin,* Combat Poverty Agency, p. 36.
42 Gaffney, Maureen (April 2010) 'Statement from Dr Maureen Gaffney on the dissolution of the NESF', available at: http://www.nesc.ie/en/our-organisation/nesf/dissolution-statement/.
43 *Oireachtas Brief,* 31 March 2010, 'Closure of the National Economic and Social Forum (NESF), available at: http://www.oireachtasbrief.ie/issues/issue-1/closure-of-the-national-economic-and-social-forum-nesf/.
44 *Irish Independent,* 26 December 2012, 'Kenny vows to back abolition of Seanad in referendum next year', available at: http://www.independent.ie/national-news/ kenny-vows-to-back-abolition-of-seanad-in-referendum-next-year-3335910.html.
45 Interview F, *op.cit.*
46 Interview L (16/09/09) Department of the Taoiseach.
47 Interview N (February 2006) Small Firms Association.
48 Hughes, I., Clancy, P., Harris, C. and Beetham, D. (2007) *Power to the People? Assessing Democracy in Ireland,* Dublin: TASC, p. 440.
49 Mair, Peter (2010) 'Paradoxes and problems of modern Irish politics', paper presented to *McGill Summer School: reforming the Republic,* July 2010.
50 Murphy, Mary P. (2012) 'Participation and deliberation: a case study of claiming our future' in, Carney, G.M and Harris, C. (eds.) *Citizens' Voices: Experiments in Democratic Renewal and Reform,* Dublin: PSAI/ ICSG/ IRCHSS.
51 Murphy, 2012, *op. cit.*
52 Murphy, 2012, *op. cit.,* p. 27.
53 Ibid.
54 *The Irish Times,* 11 November 2010.
55 www.2nd-republic.ie/.

56 www.wethecitizens.ie/.
57 We the Citizens (2011) We the Citizens Speak up for Ireland Final report from the 'We the Citizens' project, available at: http://www.wethecitizens.ie/pdfs/We-the-Citizens-2011-FINAL.pdf.
58 Ibid, p. 42.
59 Hirschman, Albert O. 1970. *Exit, Voice, and Loyalty: Responses to Decline in Firms, Organizations, and States.* Cambridge, MA: Harvard University Press.
60 *Dáil Éireann Debates* Vol. 97; 17 July, 1945, columns 2569–70. For comment see Chubb, B., *Source Book of Irish Government.* Dublin: IPA, 1983, pp. 16–17.
61 *Seanad Éireann Debates* Vol. 36; 9 December, 1948, column 3.
62 *Ellis v O'Dea* (No. 1) [1989] IR 530.
63 *Report of the Constitution Review Group*. Dublin: Government Publications, 1996.
64 *Crotty v An Taoiseach* [1987] IR 713.
65 See Kelly, F., *A Guide to Early Irish Law.* Dublin: Dublin Institute for Advanced Studies, 1988.
66 Lalor, B. (ed.), *The Encyclopaedia of Ireland.* Dublin: Gill and Macmillan, 2003, p.172.
67 [1965] IR 294 (the case was heard in 1963).
68 *Norris v Attorney General* [1984] IR 36. The plaintiff subsequently won his case against Ireland in the European Court of Human Rights.
69 Re Article 26 and the Regulation of Information (Services outside the State for the Termination of Pregnancies) Bill 1995 [1995] 1 IR 1.
70 *Re A Ward of Court* [1996] 2 IR 73.
71 The Marie Fleming case, 10 January 2013: *Fleming v Ireland* (2013) IEHC 2. This decision is under appeal.
72 'The Nature and Significance of Critical Legal Studies' (1989) *Irish Law Times,* 282.

73 Bacik, I. (2004) *Kicking and Screaming*. Dublin: O'Brien Press, p. 26.
74 [2008] 2 IR 417.
75 Some areas of the Irish Constitution are explicitly put beyond judicial review, for example, the 'Directive Principles of Social Policy' in Article 45 – meant solely as guidance to the Oireachtas – as well as the President's powers.
76 See generally Lintott, Andrew *The Laws of the Roman People* Oxford: Clarendon, 1999.
77 See, for example, Articles 28.4, 28.10 and 13.3.2.
78 Rousseau, Jean-Jacques *Du Contrat Social: Principes de Droit Politique* (1762), Book II, Chapter XII.
79 See, for example, Rousseau, Jean-Jacques (1953) 'Considerations on the Government of Poland', in Watkins, Frederick *Jean-Jacques Rousseau: Political Writings,* New York: Thomas Yelsen, Chapter 13.
80 See Tushnet, Mark (1998) 'Two Versions of Judicial Supremacy', *William and Mary Law Review* 39: 945.
81 This power to strike down legislation is made explicit in Article 34.3.1 of the Irish Constitution, whereas it was inferred by the American Supreme Court in the early (and infamous) case *Marbury v Madison* (1803).
82 Pettit, Philip 'Abolition of Seanad would be significant loss to democracy', *The Irish Times*, 28 July 2012.
83 *McGee v Attorney General* [1972] IR 1.
84 See, for example, Pettit, Philip (1997) *Republicanism: a Theory of Freedom and Government,* Oxford: Clarendon Press.
85 Pettit, Philip (1996) 'Freedom as Antipower' *Ethics,* 106: 576.
86 See generally Honohan, Iseult (2002) *Civic Republicanism,* Oxford:Taylor and Francis.
87 Pettit, Philip (2005) 'The Tree of Liberty: Republicanism, American, French and Irish' *Field Day Review* 1:29.
88 Honohan, *supra,* note 12.
89 Pettit, *supra,* note 10.

90 *Supra* note 4, Book 1.
91 *O'Reilly v Limerick Corporation* [1999].
92 Pettit, *supra,* note 13.
93 Ibid.
94 Such a power existed under the Irish Free State Constitution, although it was removed by the Oireachtas and never invoked.
95 'Iceland to elect citizens' panel to re-write Constitution', The *Guardian*, November 26, 2010
96 [1995] 1 I.R. 1.
97 Articles 5, 40.1
98 Bellamy, Richard (2007) *Political Constitutionalism*, Cambridge: Cambridge University Press; Tomkins, Adam (2005) *Our Republican Constitution,* Oxford: Hart.
99 Waldron, Jeremy (1999) *Law and Disagreement,* Oxford: Clarendon, p. 291.
100 Eisgruber, Christopher (2001) 'Civic virtue and the limits of constitutionalism' *Fordham Law Review* 69: 2131–40
101 McDowell, Michael (2011) 'Dáil Gender Law Unconstitutional', *Sunday Independent*, 20 November 2011.
102 *Attorney General v Hamilton* [1993] 2 IR 250.
103 [1972] IR 1.
104 See, for example, *Roche v Roche* [2010] IESC 10.
105 Tushnet, M. (1999) *Taking the Constitution away from the Court,* Princeton: Princeton University Press.
106 Dáil Éireann Constitution, Art. 2 (c).
107 Bagehot, Walter (1867) *The English Constitution,* London: C.A. Watts & Co. Ltd, p. 65 (emphasis added).
108 Duverger suggested in 1951 that 'in 1850 no country in the world (except the United States) knew political parties in the modern sense of the word ... In 1950 parties function in most civilized nations…' See Duverger, M. (1951) *Political Parties: Their Organization and Activity in the Modern State*, B. and R. North tr., London: Metheun & Co. Ltd., p. xxiii.

109 See Sartori, G. (1976) *Parties and Party Systems: A Framework for Analysis, Volume I*, Cambridge: Cambridge University Press, p. 21.

110 John Manning Ward specifies the debate on Robert Peel's motion of no confidence in Lord Melbourne's Whig government as the definitive episode completing this shift. See Ward, J. *Colonial Self-Government: The British Experience 1759–1856* (London: Macmillan, 1976), pp. 172–208. Gillian Peele suggests that in the eighteenth century the 'authority of the cabinet was still derived from the sovereign and the continuation of a government was dependent on the sovereign's good will rather than on the ministry being able to command parliamentary support ... Only in the nineteenth century did the Crown lose the power to choose who should become prime minister and to veto ministers to whom the monarch objected.' See Peele, G. (1995) *Governing the UK*, 3rd ed., Oxford: Blackwell Publishers, p. 92.

111 William IV was the last monarch to dismiss a Prime Minister who continued to enjoy the confidence of the House of Commons when, in 1834, he dismissed Lord Melbourne. He appointed Robert Peel despite Peel not enjoying the support of a majority of the Commons.

112 It is worth noting that as Bagehot wrote *The English Constitution* in 1867, the system he was describing was in the process of changing dramatically. He suggested, for instance, that the House of Commons 'lives in a state of perpetual choice' and that 'at any moment it can choose a ruler and dismiss a ruler'. See Bagehot (1867), p. 158. Notably, in the period between 1832 and 1867 no less than seven cabinets had been replaced by the House of Commons, that is, without an intervening general election.

113 Walsh proposed that that executive power would be vested in Ministers assisted by committees of the Dáil. The

motion went as follows: 'Whereas Mr. de Valera has repeatedly publicly announced in America that the Constitution of the Irish Republic was based on the democratic foundations underlying the Constitution of the United States; and whereas the latter body provides for the consideration of all phases of legislative activity through the medium of Committees whose findings are subject only to the veto of the whole Parliament ... and as no such machinery has yet been set up within the Irish Republican Government, with the consequent practically entire exclusion of three-fourths of the people's representatives from effective work on the nation's behalf, we now resolve to bring this Constitution into harmony with the American idea of Committees elected by the whole House, and clothed with similar powers ...' As quoted in Ward, A. J. (1994) *The Irish Constitutional Tradition: Responsible Government and Modern Ireland, 1782–1992,* Dublin: Irish Academic Press, p. 159.

114 See Dáil Éireann, *Debates*, vol. 1, 5 October, 1922, col. 1271.

115 The German scholar Leo Kohn wrote that the 1922 document 'reduced to precise terms the conventional rules of the British Constitution.' See Kohn, L. (1932) *The Constitution of the Irish Free State,* London: George Allen & Unwin Ltd, p. 80.

116 Rather, his enthusiasm had to do with setting the polity in a Catholic frame and, to an even greater extent, with aiming a final kick at the Anglo–Irish Treaty that he had so dreaded.

117 In Basil Chubb's words, he 'found the system which he inherited an adequate instrument for his purposes and, indeed, well suited to a strong prime minister leading a loyal majority party that looked to him for initiative and direction'. Chubb, B. (1978) *The Constitution and Constitutional Change in Ireland*, Dublin: Institute of Public Administration, p. 32.

118 Constitution of Ireland, Article 13.1.1 and Article 13.1.2 (emphasis added).

119 This is, of course, a simplified account. For a detailed historical analysis, see M. Gallagher, (2009) 'The Oireachtas: President and Parliament' in Coakley, J. and Gallagher, M. (eds.), *Politics in the Republic of Ireland* Oxford: Routledge, pp. 204–207.

120 Governments in Britain were defeated on votes of confidence on only three occasions in the twentieth century: twice in 1924 and again in 1979. See Turpin, C. and Tomkins, A. (2011) *British Government and the Consti tution*, Cambridge: Cambridge University Press, p. 568. Similarly, the Dáil did actually 'bring down' a government on two occasions, while it should be acknowledged that governments have often 'jumped before they were pushed.' The argument is not that parliament is impotent in this regard. It is merely that they are much less potent in practice than in theory.

121 Chubb suggests that government ministers have a 'virtual monopoly of initiating legislation and other policy proposals …'. See Chubb, B. (1992) *The Government and Politics of Ireland*, London: Longman, p. 158.

122 Basil Chubb makes the point in his aptly entitled chapter. See Chubb, B. (1988) 'Constitutional Myth and Political Practice' in Farrell, B. (ed.) *De Valera's Constitution and Ours,* Dublin: Gill and Macmillan.

123 This snapshot relies on Gallagher, 'The Oireachtas: President and Parliament' in Coakley and Gallagher (2009), p. 230–232.

124 Tomkins, A. (2005) *Our Republican Constitution*, Oxford: Hart Publishing, pp. 2–3 (emphasis added).

125 Tomkins (2005), p. 2.

126 Ibid.

127 See Houses of the Oireachtas, 'A Brief Guide to How Your Parliament Works', available at http://www.oireachtas.ie/parliament/media/michelle/parliamentworks/Parliamentary-Guide-Eng-(web).pdf [accessed 27 December 2012].

128 See for example, Dooney, S. and O'Toole, J. (2009) *Irish Government Today,* Dublin: Gill and Macmillan, Chapters 1-3, M. MacCarthaigh, *Accountability in Irish Parliamentary Politics* (Dublin: Institute of Public Administration, 2005), Chapter 4.

129 See The Report of the Tribunal of Inquiry into the Beef Processing Industry (Dublin: Statutory Office, 1994), as quoted in F. O'Toole (1995) *Meanwhile Back at the Ranch: The Politics of Irish Beef,* London: Vintage, p. 241.

130 See O'Toole (1994), p. 241.

131 Shane Martin's analysis of PQs between 1997 and 2002 finds that 55% of them do *not* have a constituency basis. By any measure, this suggests that a disproportionate number concern constituency issues, given that the parliament is concerned, fundamentally, with national laws and policies. See Martin, S. 'Monitoring Irish Government' in O'Malley, E. (ed.) (2012), *Governing Ireland* (Dublin: Institute of Public Administration).

132 See F. O'Toole (2010) *Enough is Enough: How to Build a New Republic* Dublin: Penguin, pp. 67–70.

133 See Gallagher, 'The Oireachtas: President and Parliament' in Coakley and Gallagher (2009), p. 232.

134 See Oireachtas Joint, Select and Standing Committees for the 31st Dáil and 23rd Seanad, at http://www.oireachtas.ie/parliament/oireachtasbusiness/committees_list/ [accessed 27 December 2012].

135 On the functions of convenors, see Houses of the Oireachtas, Fact Sheet 2: The Role and Work of Oireachtas

Committees, available at http://www.oireachtas.ie/parliament/media/committees/factsheets/Fact-Sheet-2-The-Role-and-Work-of-Oireachtas-Committees-without-codes.pdf [accessed December 27, 2012], p. 8. Martin suggests that 'the allocation of committee chairs, although perhaps formally an issue for each individual committee, seems to be decided in negotiations more centrally among Party Whips ...'. See Martin, 'The Committee System' in MacCathaigh and Manning (eds.) (2010), *The Houses of the Oireachtas: Parliament in Ireland*, Dublin: Institute of Public Administration.

136 The idea was provided for in Article 55 of the Free State Constitution. In a modern version, it could be that the Dáil (through an impartially representative committee of the Dáil) would be empowered to appoint ministers from outside of party politics (and who would not be members of the Dáil) to run certain Departments of State (e.g., education, health, tourism, etc.). Unlike members of the Cabinet, the extern minister would not be subject to collective Cabinet responsibility. They could therefore run their departments without excessive concern for the general government line. The Parliament would be enhanced as it could freely approve or disapprove reform proposals brought before it by the extern ministers. If a proposal were defeated, the government would not collapse; the minister would simply return with a better proposal that might attract the support of the parliamentarians. In other words, the Parliament would control the external ministers in a real way. The idea failed in the 1920s for various reasons, not least the amendment to an earlier draft that allowed that extern ministers could be members of the Dáil. This meant that all such ministers appointed in the 1920s were party men and members of

the Dáil. For a good account, see Cahillane, L. (2012) 'Anti-Party Politics in the Irish Free State Constitution', *Dublin University Law Journal*, 19: 34.

137 The expenses scandal of 2009 seemed to be the 'rupture' that prompted Westminster power-wielders to accept the importance of institutional reform that would result in the holding of power to account. The so-called Wright Committee Report, chaired by the academic and parliamentarian Tony Wright, was appointed to make reform proposals. The report is available online. See House of Commons Reform Committee: First Report of Session 2008–09, 'Rebuilding the House', available at http://www.publications.parliament.uk/pa/cm200809/cmselect/cmrefhoc/1117/111702.htm [accessed 27 December 2012].

138 *This is my Constitution*, p. 1. D'Arcy, Kathy (Ungovernable Bodies), copy made available to NWCI.

139 'How women were 'put in their place', Ferriter, Diarmaid, *Irish Independent*, 12 December 2012.

140 Programme of first Dáil, accessed via www.firstdail.com

141 The contents of this paper, then, are based on the policies of the National Women's Council of Ireland, which comprises 170 local and national women's organisations. The mandate is given by the membership and policies are set at an AGM where motions are voted on. In addition, in September 2012, a specific process of consultation (including a meeting of Members held in Cork and a period of written consultation) was undertaken by the NWCI in developing policies relating to the Constitution. Thus the views expressed here represent the considered views of a diverse group of women from across Ireland representing different social and ethnic perspectives in our society.

142 Judt, Tony (2011)*Ill fares the land*, London: Penguin, pp. 21–22

143 Brady, Alan D. P. (2012) *The Constitution, Gender and Reform: Improving the position of women in the Irish Constitution*, Dublin: NWCI, p. 56.
144 Petit, Philip (2004) 'From Republican Theory to Public Policy' in Jones, Mary (ed.) *The Republic: Essays from RTÉ Radio's The Thomas Davis Lecture Series*, Dublin: RTÉ, p. 135.
145 Lynch, Kathleen, Baker, John and Cantillon, Sara (2001) *Equality: frameworks for change*, Dublin: UCD, p. 19, accessed online via http://hdl.handle.net/10197/2045.
146 Committee on the Elimination of Discrimination Against Women, Thirty-Third Session, Concluding Comments: Ireland CEDAW/C/IRL/CO/4-5 at paras. 24–25.
147 Slaughter, Anne Marie (2012) 'Why Women Still Can't Have it All', *The Atlantic*, accessed online http://www.theatlantic.com/magazine/archive/2012/07/why-women-still-cant-have-it-all/309020/.
148 'Women and Men in Ireland 2011', Dublin, CSO 2012, p. 19.
149 Quarter 1, 2012, Quarterly National Household Survey (QNHS), Dublin, CSO 2012.
150 Derived from Census 2011.
151 'Our Bill of Health', Dublin, CSO, 2012
152 'Our Bill of Health', Dublin, CSO, 2012, p. 57
153 The question asked was, 'Do you provide regular unpaid personal help for a friend or family member with a long-term illness, health problem or disability?'
154 'Who cares? Challenging the Myths about Gender and Care in Ireland', Dublin, NWCI, 2009.
155 Ibid.
156 CSO (2012) EU SILC 2010
157 Brady, Alan D. P. (2012) *The Constitution, Gender and Reform: Improving the Position of Women in the Irish Constitution*, Dublin: NWCI, p. 82.

158 Engster, D. (2005) 'Rethinking Care Theory: The Practice of Caring and the Obligation to Care', *Hypatia* 20: 63–64, cited in Brady, Alan D. P. (2012) *The Constitution, Gender and Reform: Improving the Position of Women in the Irish Constitution*, Dublin, NWCI, p. 41.

159 Baker, J., Lynch, K., Cantillon, S. and Walsh, J., *Equality from Theory to Action*, London, Macmillan, 2004.

160 O'Connor , O. and Dunne, C. (2006) 'Valuing Unpaid Care Work' in O'Connor, T. and Murphy, M. (eds.) *Social Care in Ireland: Theory, Policy and Practice*, Cork: CIT Press.

161 Murphy, Mary P. (2012) *Careless to Careful Activation: Making Activation Work for Women*. Dublin, NWCI and SIPTU.

162 Brady, Alan D. P. (2012) *The Constitution, Gender and Reform: Improving the position of women in the Constitution*, Dublin: NWCI, p. 42.

163 Ibid. p. 40. Ref: [2001] 4 IR 259.

164 Ibid. p. 43. Ref:[1985] SCC (3) 545.

165 Alan D. P. (2012) *The Constitution, Gender and Reform: Improving the position of women in the Constitution*, Dublin: NWCI, p. 96.

166 Ibid. p. 42. Ref: (2000) 11 BCLR 1169

167 Ibid. p. 43. Ref: (2002) 10 BCLR 1033 (CC)

168 Ibid. p. 44.

169 ICESCR Article 11

170 ICESCR Article 12.

171 ICESCR Article 1.

172 Inter-Parliamentary Union (2012) Women in National Parliaments: The Situation as of 30 July 2013. Retrieved from http://www.ipu.org/wmn-e/classif.htm.

173 Brady, Alan D. P. (2012) *The Constitution, Gender and Reform: Improving the position of women in the Constitution*, Dublin: NWCI.

174 Cornwall, Andrea (2008) *Democratising Engagement: What the UK Can Learn from International Experience*, London: Demos, p. 23.

175 Presentation given to NWCI member's meeting on the Constitution by Dr Laura Cahillane, Department of Government, UCC. Available on www.nwci.ie .

176 For further details cf. *Report on Reasons Behind Voter Behaviour in the Oireachtas Inquiry Referendum 2011* (Department of Public Expenditure and Reform, January 2012), at p. 26.

177 Ireland's severe levels of under-representation of women in politics are exacerbated when one observes the annual slide in our world ranking, particularly when countries who come in tied places are included. Ireland's status in the Inter-Parliamentary Union ranking is now 106th country in the world, making us the third-worst performer in the EU.

178 Brady, Alan D. P. (2012) *The Constitution, Gender and Reform: Improving the position of women in the Constitution*, Dublin: NWCI, p. 28.

179 Norris, P. (1997) 'Choosing Electoral Systems: Proportional, Majoritarian and Mixed Systems', *International Political Science Review* 18: 297. It should be noted that in some countries where PR systems bring high levels of female representation, other factors, such as candidate quotas, are also in use.

180 McLeay, E. (2006) 'Climbing On: Rules, values and women's representation in the New Zealand Parliament' in Sawer, M., Tremblay, M. and Trimble, L. (eds.) 'Introduction: Patterns and practice in the parliamentary representation of women' in Sawyer, M, Tremblay, M and Trimble, L. *Representing Women in Parliament: A Comparative Study*, London: Routledge, at pp.74–76.

181 Bacik, I. (2004) *Kicking and Screaming: Dragging Ireland*

into the 21st Century, Dublin: O'Brien Press, Dublin, p. 242.

182 Brady, Alan D. P. (2012) *The Constitution, Gender and Reform: Improving the position of women in the Constitution*, Dublin: NWCI, p. 75.

183 Offences Against the Person Act 1861.

184 In 1992, in what became known as the *X* case, the Attorney General was granted an injunction to prevent a 14-year-old girl who was pregnant as a result of rape from seeking an abortion abroad. This injunction was appealed to the Supreme Court, which gave its interpretation of Article 40.3.3 and held that the Constitution guarantees the right to terminate a pregnancy lawfully and within the State where there is a real and substantial risk to the life of the mother (as distinct from her health), which can only be averted by terminating the pregnancy. It stated that a risk of suicide may constitute a real and substantial risk to life. *Attorney General v X and Others* [1992] 1 IR 1.

185 Red C and the *Sunday Business Post*, December 2012, http://www.businesspost.ie/#!story/Home/News/Red+C+poll%3A+majority+demand+X+case+legislation/id/78241919-150b-a2a0-577f-97741195800.

186 ICCP-2010 defines a crisis pregnancy as a pregnancy that represents a personal crisis or an emotional trauma in either of the following circumstances: (a) a pregnancy that began as a crisis or (b) a pregnancy that develops into a crisis before the birth due to a change in circumstances. A pregnancy, planned or unplanned, can become a crisis pregnancy for a range of complex personal, social and economic reasons, including concern about the well-being of other children, diagnosis of serious foetal abnormality, financial worries, pre-existing health problems, including mental health problems, and relationship issues (McBride, Orla, Morgan, Karen and McGee, Hannah. Crisis Pregnancy Programme Report No. 24, Irish Contraception

and Crisis Pregnancy Study 2010 (ICCP-2010), A Survey of the General Population).

187 McBride, Orla, Morgan, Karen and McGee, Hannah. Crisis Pregnancy Programme Report No. 24, Irish Contraception and Crisis Pregnancy Study 2010 (ICCP-2010), A Survey of the General Population

188 Department of Health (2012) *Abortion Statistics, England and Wales: 2011*: http://transparency.dh.gov.uk/2012/05/29/abortion-statistics-2011/ [accessed 17 September 2012]

189 According to statistics compiled by the HSE Crisis Pregnancy Programme, 1,470 women travelled from Ireland to the Netherlands from 2005 to 2009 to access safe abortion services. See further: http://www.crisispregnancy.ie/news/number-of-women-giving-irish-addresses-at-uk-abortion-clinics-decreases-for-tenth-year-in-a-row-according-to-depa rtment-of-health-uk/

190 Irish Family Planning Association: Abortion Statistics. http://www.ifpa.ie/Hot-Topics/Abortion/Statistics

191 Singh, S. et al (2009)*Abortion Worldwide: A Decade of Uneven Progress*, New York: Guttmacher Institute.

192 Brady, Alan D. P. (2012) *The Constitution, Gender and Reform: Improving the position of women in the Constitution*, Dublin: NWCI, p. 81.

193 *Missing Pieces: A comparison of the rights and responsibilities gained from civil partnership compared to the rights and responsibilities gained through civil marriage in Ireland,* Marriage Equality, Dublin 2011

194 [2008] 2 IR 417.

195 *Reference Re Same Sex Marriage* [2004] 3 SCR 698.

196 [1985] IR 532, at p. 536.

197 Sinn Féin were returned with 73 seats, the Home Rule party 6 and Unionist candidates 26.

198 See Mitchell, Arthur (1974) *Labour in Irish Politics,* New York, pp. 94–103.

199 See Farrell, Brian (1970–71) 'Labour and the Irish Party System: a suggested approach to analysis', *Economic and Social Review* 2: 3.
200 O Cathasaigh, Aindrias 'Getting with the programme: Labour, the Dáil and the Democratic Programme of 1919', *Red Banner,* March 2009, p.1. This is the most thorough examination of the drafting of the document.
201 O'Hegarty, P. S. (1924) *The Victory of Sinn Féin,* Dublin: University College Dublin Press, quoted in Laffan, M. (1999) *The Resurrection of Ireland: The Sinn Féin Party, 1916–1923*, Cambridge: Cambridge University Press, p. 214.
202 O'Faolain, Seán (1965) *Vive Moi! An autobiography,* London, pp.145–6.
203 Laffan, M. (1999) *The Resurrection of Ireland: The Sinn Féin Party, 1916–1923*, Cambridge: Cambridge University Press, p. 214.
204 Quoted in ibid. p. 2
205 This is the accepted course of events, although over the years there were various claims made regarding the authorship (notably, in November 1944, Sean T. O'Kelly told the Seanad that he wrote it, although Johnson and the others had given him some notes). See O' Shannon, Cathal, 'The 1919 Democratic Programme. I' in *The Irish Times* 31 January 1944 (this was the first in a three-part series by O' Shannon on the drafting, content and reading of the programme published in the *The Irish Times* 31 January–2 February 1944)
206 *The Irish Times* 31 January 1944
207 *The Irish Times* 21 January 1969
208 *The Irish Times* 31 January 1944; interview with Cathal O' Shannon featured in 'The First Dáil', first broadcast by Raidió Éireann 19 January 1969.
209 The text of Johnson's original document was first published on 1 February 1944 in *The Irish Times.*

210 O Cathasaigh, Aindrias 'Getting with the programme: Labour, the Dáil and the Democratic Programme of 1919', *Red Banner,* March 2009, p. 3.

211 P. S. O' Hegarty (1952) *A History of Ireland Under the Union,* London, p. 727 quoted in O Cathasaigh, Aindrias 'Getting with the programme: Labour, the Dáil and the Democratic Programme of 1919', *Red Banner,* March 2009, p. 3.

212 'The drafting of the programme' *Irish Press* 27 July 1961 quoted in O Cathasaigh, Aindrias 'Getting with the programme: Labour, the Dáil and the Democratic Programme of 1919', *Red Banner,* March 2009, p. 3

213 Ibid. It is worth bearing in mind that O' Shannon had himself been a member of the IRB. See also Mitchell, A. (1995) *Revolutionary Government in Ireland,* Dublin, p. 15

214 *The Irish Times,* 1 February 1944

215 O Cathasaigh, Aindrias 'Getting with the programme: Labour, the Dáil and the Democratic Programme of 1919', *Red Banner,* March 2009, p. 4.

216 Ibid.

217 *The Irish Times,* 2 February 1944; Gaughan, J. A. *Thomas Johnson,* p. 157

218 'An Chéad Dáil 1919,' first broadcast on Teilifís Éireann 20 January 1969

219 Beaslaí, P. (1926) *Michael Collins and the making of a new Ireland Volume 1*, Dublin, p. 259 quoted in O Cathasaigh, Aindrias 'Getting with the programme: Labour, the Dáil and the Democratic Programme of 1919', *Red Banner,* March 2009, p. 4.

220 DD 11 April 1919, Vol. 1 Col. 78

221 O'Connor, E. (2004) *The Reds and the Green. Ireland, Russia and the Communist Internationals 1919–43,* Dublin, p. 73

222 For the drafting of the Free State constitution see 'The drafting of the Irish Free State Constitution, parts I-IV' *The Irish Jurist* 5–6 (1970–71).
223 DD 25 September 1922 Volume 1 Col 696.
224 DD 25 September 1922 Volume 1 Col 701.
225 For example, Pataud, E. and Pouget, E., *Syndicalism and the Co-operative Commonwealth* (1913, Pluto Press 1990).
226 Morrisey, Thomas J. (2013) 'William Martin Murphy, the employers and 1913' in Devine, Francis (ed.) *1913. A Capital in Conflict: Dublin City and the 1913 Lockout,* Dublin: Four Courts Press, p.169.
227 Laffan, Michael (1999)*The Resurrection of Ireland: The Sinn Féin Party 1916–1923.* Cambridge: Cambridge University Press, p. 214.
228 Regan, John M. (1999)*The Irish Counter-Revolution 1921–1936,* Dublin: Gill & Macmillan, p. 148.
229 DD 25 September 1922 Volume 1 Col 709–10.
230 *The Irish Times* 21 January 1969.
231 *The Irish Times* 14 August 1964.
232 *The Irish Times* 13 August 1964; 10 October 1966.
233 Ó Tuathaigh, Gearóid (1988) 'The Irish Nation-State in the Constitution' in Brian Farrell (ed.) *De Valera's Constitution and Ours,* Dublin: Gill & Macmillan, p. 55
234 Subsequently, Skeffington complained that the only reference to his question in the official report amounted to '*chuir an Seanadóir Mac Síthigh-Sceimhealtún isteach ar na cúrsaí i mBéarla*' (see SD 5 March 1969, Vol 66, col 422), taking exception to the redaction of his remarks and the rather odd Gaelicisation of his name. The later version of the official report removed any reference to his interjection.
235 *The Irish Times* 25 January 1989.
236 Professor Murphy also told the house that it had only been drafted at the behest of the IRB, an error noted by Mary

Holland (*The Irish Times* 25 January 1989). Professor Murphy wrote to the paper acknowledging his mistake and the official report was corrected to read 'against the wishes of the IRB'. (SD 18 January 1989, 121 Col 1625).

237 DD 25 January 2011 Vol 727 Cols 442–446.

238 *The Irish Times* 7 August 2012.

239 SD 6 April 1982 Vol 97 Col 495.